FABRIC LANDSCAPES
BY MACHINE

❧ Linda Crone ❧

Published by

Krause Publishing
700 E. State St.
Iola, WI 54990-0001
Telephone 715-445-2214
www.krause.com

Please call or write for our free catalog. Our toll-free number to place an order
or obtain a free catalog is 800-258-0929 or please use our regular business telephone 715-445-2214 for editorial comment and further information.

The following product or company names appear in this book:
505® by Odif, American Traditional Stencils, Artist's Color Wheel© by The
Color Wheel Co., Cactus Punch Signature Series "Landscape Elements," Delta
Ceramcoat, Foliage by Robert Kaufman, Glitter Superior Threads, HeatnBond
Lite®, Hero Arts, Hi-Fashion Fabrics, Inc., Husqvarna Dissolve-A-Way™,
Husqvarna Tear-A-Way™ Stabilizer, Kreinik, Madeira Avalon®, Madeira
Décor 6, Madeira Glamour, Madeira Jewel, P & B Textiles, Posh Impressions,
Quilt Sew Easy Flexible Hoop, Quiltgard™, Rubber Stampede, Shiva Artist's
Paintstik Oil Colors, Staedtler, Stitch-N-Tear® by Pellon®, Sulky® KK
2000™, Sulky Sliver™, Sulky Solvy™, Sulky Tear-Easy™ Stabilizer, Sulli-
vans Temporary Spray Adhesive, Superior Glitter, The Stencil Collection,
Ultrasuede, Wonder Under Light Fusible Web, YLI Candlelight, YLI Monet,
YLI Pearl Crown Rayon.

Library of Congress Catalog Number: 99-68135

ISBN: 0-87341-836-0

Printed in the United States of America

Dedication

I am grateful for…

My husband John—for giving me the freedom and support to pursue my interests in sewing as a career. This book would not have been possible without you. Thank you for your help with the reading and editing process, and for enduring all the hours it took to make this book happen.

My son Nathan—whose gift with words said it best. "I guess I shouldn't be surprised you're going into sewing, for I don't know anyone else's mom who makes everything in the house." Thank you for helping me see more clearly my gifts.

My daughter Tricia—for showing so much love and interest in all that I do, even though we don't share the love of sewing! Thank you for being a great model, so much fun to be with, and for that terrific smile that always brightens my day.

My mother Violetta—for the many hours you spent sitting by my side, and encouraging me to sew as a child. Thank you for helping me to develop my interests and abilities during those formative years.

My dog Chelsea — for her constant companionship and supervision of everything happening in the sewing room.

Acknowledgments

I would especially like to thank all my students who have taken my classes and have encouraged me to write this book. Your eagerness for more knowledge has helped to propel me along the way.

My special thanks to my editor, Barbara Case. Your vision, insight, and guidance have been very instrumental to the success of this book. Thank you for your patience and the opportunity to work with you. I appreciate all the wonderful folks at Krause Publications. You have all been great to work with.

My special thanks to Judy Brekhus for all of the hours of your time you have generously given. You were right, the landscapes had potential!

My special thanks to Betty VanBriesen, and all of the hours you have put in sewing. I have enjoyed working with you and creating some really fun landscapes together.

Many thanks to those who have contributed landscapes or garments. You have made this book all the more special with your contributions: Patsy Shields, Betty VanBriesen, Nancy Wheat, Luetta Peters, Diane Miller, and Marge Albrecht

A special thanks to my friend, Judy Gambrel, for encouraging me years ago to do something with my sewing abilities.

I would also like to say a special thanks to Jerry Binfet for all your support and encouraging words each step of the way.

A very special thanks to Cactus Punch and your gifted staff, for the beautiful digitized designs. It was an honor to work with all of you to develop the "Landscape Elements" embroidery designs. Your quality work is a shining example in this book.

A special thanks to my sewing peers who have been encouraging, and shared their words of wisdom with me: Linda McGehee, Nancy Cornwell, Linda Vivian, Kay Wood, and Nancy Zieman. I am grateful for your support.

I would also like to say many thanks to my photographer, Jim Orlando. I really appreciate all of your creative abilities and attention to detail. Thank you for your significant contribution in making this a colorful book.

I would like to thank my family for hanging in there with me through this process. Especially my husband John who coined the phrase, "What are you doing, working on your book?" Thank you Tricia, for your willingness to take time out of your busy schedule and come home to model garments for this book. Also, many thanks to Karen Bryant, my daughter-in-law, for your willingness to pitch in and help when I needed some backup.

I am especially thankful for the companies who have been supportive with products and equipment.

Fabric:
  Michael Miller Fabrics
  Robert Kaufman
  Hoffman California Fabrics
  Hi-Fashion Fabrics Inc.
  Bali Fabrications
  P & B Textiles
  Rosebar

Threads:
  Madeira
  Kreinik Mfg. Co. Inc.
  Sulky of America
  Superior Threads
  YLI Corp.

Sewing Machines:
  Bernina of America, Inc.
  American Sales Corp.
  Viking Sewing Machine Inc.

American Traditional Stencils
Cactus Punch Embroidery Digitizing
Heritage Handcrafts
Thread PRO
Omnigrid, Inc.

I am most thankful for all of you who have been so willing to help, and I hope that I have not overlooked anyone. Although this book only has one author, it really takes a team of people to make this publication possible. My heartfelt thanks go out to all of you.

Foreword

Some of my fondest memories as a child are of hiking the hills of North Carolina and West Virginia with my parents, brothers, sister, and friends. We spent many a weekend or vacation exploring nature, picking daisies on my grandparents' farm, walking in the creeks of Mississippi, and shuffling leaves under our feet on an autumn walk. As an adult, I enjoy these same pleasures with my husband. We have traveled the globe by air, van, car, motorcycle, bicycle, and on foot to view and enjoy this wonderful world of ours.

Linda Crone allows us to capture these moments with textiles. She has the ability to combine a variety of printed or solid fabrics together with decorative threads to duplicate a special scene from nature or create an imaginative one. Her easy manner and simplified techniques are the key to her success. She can show the beginner as well as the most advanced stitcher her uncomplicated manner of manipulating fabrics, combining textures, and blending threads to transform fabric into art. By using color variety, she shows how nature transforms a scene from spring to summer to fall to winter and back.

Linda takes detail to another level. She has designed an embroidery disk to achieve the special balance of hills and water with flowers, boats, and bridges. Her disk, digitized by Cactus Punch, allows the thread artist to stitch their best by fine tuning detail. Free motion is an option, not a necessity.

Whether to wear, frame for the wall, send as a greeting card, decorate a pillow or bag, *Fabric Landscapes by Machine* allows those of us who like to sew and quilt the opportunity to create the ideal scene and seize a special moment in time.

by Linda McGehee, author of *Creating Texture with Textiles*

Table of Contents

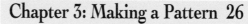

Introduction

my love of sewing started when I was about ten years old, growing up in a small Iowa town. I could sit for hours making clothes for my dolls out of nothing but a few scraps. As I got older, I enjoyed making clothes for myself. Even though my mother didn't sew much, she would sit beside me and together we would read the pattern directions over and over, trying to figure out what they meant. Since then, I have sewn a little bit of everything: curtains, pillows, bedspreads, a bridal dress, prom dresses, men's suits, purses—you name it. My real passion for sewing is designing landscapes and wearable art garments. I am a self-taught artist who has learned to trust the sense of color and design within myself. I know what I like when I see it.

Several years ago I purchased my first sewing machine—one that could do all those wonderful decorative stitches. Choosing one was difficult because there were so many wonderful models available. Part of the fun was studying all the features and comparing the bells and whistles each had to offer. I pondered the decision carefully and thought about it for quite some time before I purchased one. I am a careful spender and wanted to make sure I could justify my purchase once it was made. But as soon as I had the new machine, I knew the fun was about to begin!

Much of the focus of my work has been on finding ways to utilize all those wonderful stitches this new technology has delivered to our sewing rooms. Designing and sewing landscapes has provided a wonderful canvas to express the endless possibilities for their use.

One of the most frequent questions I am asked by sewers as I travel, teach, and exhibit at sewing shows and stores is, "How did you get started creating landscapes?" Many new adventures in this world come about due to necessity. I would have to say that this was the case for me. The office where I used to work moved to a new location with very bare walls. I had that same uncomfortable feeling you get when you move into a new home, knowing it won't be complete until you get the accessories out and the pictures hung on the walls. I decided to create a landscape for the entryway and that's how my journey to discovering the potential for all those decorative stitches began.

This book will show you how to design landscapes, beginning with finding inspiration and ending with finishing touches. I'll share with you the important design elements, how to work with decorative stitches and threads, special embellishment techniques, and lots of pictures for inspiration. I've also included some fast and easy landscape patterns to help set you in motion. You'll soon be ready to go on to bigger and better things! Please feel free to send me pictures of your endeavors!

I hope that the many hours I have spent on my journey exploring landscapes will be beneficial to you as you read this book. I want to inspire you to look within yourself and be all that you can be.

Kind Regards,

Linda Crone

My daughter, Tricia Bryant (right) and I. This was the first photo taken for the book and Tricia is wearing the first landscape jacket I created.

Chapter 1

Finding Inspiration

Where does inspiration come from? How do you get started? My students often ask me where I find my ideas and I have no pat answer. Sometimes I wonder myself where I come up with ideas! I am often unsure of how to answer that question because there is no specific direction I can point them to find ideas. Inspiration can come from almost anywhere and it is different things for everyone. We are all such unique individuals—what inspires one person may not even turn someone else's head.

I believe inspiration and ideas often come when you least expect them. Be ready. You may see something when you're shopping, driving, watching television, or going for a walk. Pay attention when mother nature unfolds a beautiful sunrise for you, or a sunset or snowfall. Take note of the flowers popping open to say hello in the spring and study their fascinating colors. I always carry paper and pencil with me in case I want to write something down or draw a little sketch. I keep a file of ideas and pencil sketches to refresh my memory of things that were of particular interest. For me, most of the time my inspiration comes from an intriguing fabric that jump starts my batteries and gets the creative juices flowing.

When I started designing my first landscape, I wasn't sure where to begin. Luckily, I have a picture in my home that inspired me and became the starting point for my design. It is a beautiful landscape titled "Sandmarkings" that was created from handmade papers by M.P. Marion of Racine, Wisconsin. I spent a lot of time studying this picture and decided I could make something along the same lines using fabric instead of paper. It appeared to me that the artist began by layering the papers, starting with the sky at the top, then working her way to the bottom.

I had the privilege of visiting with the artist when I called to get her permission to show

"Sandmarkings" by M.P. Marion. This handmade paper landscape inspired me to begin my first fabric landscape.

"Sandmarkings" in my book. I discovered that she first started creating landscapes from fabric, then changed her medium to handmade papers. Life is interesting, isn't it? Ms. Marion was very interested to learn that her artwork inspired me to achieve a similar look with fabric. And so it goes!

Pictured here is my first effort at developing a landscape. It was designed for the bare-walled office I mentioned in the Introduction. The color scheme in the room was primarily teal and burgundy. You can see the resemblance to "Sandmarkings," especially in the trees that were free-motion stitched. There is an interesting assortment of fabrics in this scene. I just started cutting pieces of fabric at random, working from top to bottom. The fabric for the water is a foiled knit typically used for holiday wear or formal occasions—it makes a dazzling reflective water fabric. I also used a couple pieces of home decorator fabrics that have a little more weight and texture to them.

For the foreground I used a very light-weight polyester blouse fabric. I stitched the basic construction of the landscape with a simple zigzag stitch and monofilament thread in the needle. So, those of you who don't have a machine with a lot of fancy stitches needn't be dismayed. Here is a great example of what you can do without those stitches.

There are many places to look for inspiration and ideas for landscapes. I enjoy taking a stroll through a wildlife art gallery and looking at the paintings. There you will also find coffee table books by artists with their signature collection of paintings. These are wonderful books to thumb through for

My first landscape made with randomly selected fabrics and a simple zigzag stitch.

a new idea. Many art galleries give away catalogs and flyers with lots of photos of current and upcoming releases of prints. Your local bookstore is a great source for calendars and books about nature. Some of the most beautiful landscapes are featured on calendars. Look through magazines such as *National Geographic*, outdoor sporting issues, and travel books for beautiful landscapes. I always keep my eyes open for landscape postcards and greeting cards when we travel. Your family photo album may also contain pictures of vacations or a family farm that would be a great beginning for a landscape. I have also found landscapes in books and software programs featuring clip art. As you can see, there are numerous sources for landscape inspiration available at your fingertips. Make it a mental priority to be on the lookout for them!

I enjoy watching children with crayons. They have a wonderful imagination and a free creative spirit. They are relaxed and just have fun. We can learn a lot from observing what they do, as most of us have forgotten how to play. Creativity is not something that can be forced. We must give ourselves permission to play and try not to worry about ruining the fabric. There is more fabric where that came from!

Our schedules and lives are too hurried and it seems there is so much to do in so little time. I encourage you to slow down, relax, and enjoy the process of sewing. Do what it takes to loosen up when it's time to sew—turn on some music or enjoy a cup of coffee. Don't set deadlines for the completion date of a project—a deadline can lead to disaster because you are trying to force creativity. Be patient with yourself and realize that you are going to make some goofs. It's okay—learn from mistakes and make them part of the process of becoming better at what you're doing. Goofs can turn into wonderful new discoveries! I have spent many hours with my seam ripper in hand. Try not to get frustrated with yourself because this will bring your creativity to a halt.

Most of all, believe in yourself. No one else can do this for you, it must come from within. Be careful what you say to yourself, your "self talk" I call it. And don't take on anyone else's "stinkin thinkin" that brings you down either. Unfortunately, a lot of talent is wasted because of what we say to ourselves or what someone else says to us that undermines our self esteem. If you believe you can do something, you will. If you think you can't, you won't. I have taught many hands-on classes and know that there's a difference when a student says "I'll try" instead of "I can." It's just that simple.

I have spent many years in sales observing people. The amazing thing is that the finish line is the same distance for all of us. It's not always the ones who are the smartest or most gifted or talented who win the race. Some see obstacles where others see opportunities. Choose friends who are positive and upbeat. Negative influences are too draining on your energy levels and life is too short for that.

The Design Process

Where Does the Design Process Begin?

One question I often hear is, "How can I pull fabrics together to design a landscape?" My answer is that the design process for constructing a landscape can begin at several different points. I like to refer to this as the "point of origin." It is similar to decorating a room in your home. Do you start with the carpet, furniture, bedspread, or a decorator fabric? Or when you make a new garment, do you start with the pattern, fabric, an interesting button, or just an idea? The point of origin in designing a landscape may take off from many different angles. Landscapes are like any other project in that there are several ways to "enter" into the design process.

Following are some possible points of origin for designing a landscape. You will probably develop your own after you've read through these.

Garment Fabric

Many of the wearable art garments I design feature a landscape on the back. These are truly unique pieces of clothing. I believe I have more requests for pictures of my backside than my front! If you use the base garment fabric as your point of origin, you can then choose the other fabrics for the landscape to coordinate with that base fabric. The objective is to find fabrics that enhance what you started with.

The jacket on page 13 always gets rave reviews. The base fabric in the sleeves is a Robert Kaufman fabric called "Foliage." It has a very eye-catching collection of leaves in blues, greens, purples, wine, and a little teal. All my favorite colors! When you design a landscape around a garment fabric, that fabric becomes key to the design process. The garment fabric sets the theme for the colors of the landscape, leading you to make fabric selections for the three most crucial areas of the landscape: sky, midground, and foreground. Once you've chosen a fabric for the garment, you can then select fabrics for these three areas that will complement the garment fabric. Once these fabrics are determined, the rest is easy! It's simply a matter of finding a few fabrics that work together to fill in the gaps.

The base fabric in the sleeves was the point of origin for the fabrics in the landscape on this jacket.

Sky Fabric

Another way to begin a landscape is to find a wonderful sky fabric to use as the point of origin for the design. The sky fabric then becomes the key element to making all the fabrics work together and it is also one of the main focal points of the landscape because the eye always seeks the horizon line. There are so many great sky fabrics on the market today and they come in all kinds of patterns and color choices. I like to work with sky fabrics that have more than just white clouds and blue skies. If the sky fabric has several colors, it is much easier to pull in companion fabrics in the design process.

In this landscape the beautiful sky fabric is by Hi-Fashion Fabrics. Unfortunately, this exact fabric is no longer available, but it gives you an idea of what to look for. This fabric was a favorite of mine because of the dynamic use of many colors, thereby setting the stage for something wonderful to happen. You can see tints and shades of blue, lavender, mint green, and some white around the edges of the clouds. The color theme for this landscape was established and designed around this great sky fabric. As you walk through the fabric store, visualize how multicolored fabrics would work as sky, even if they don't have clouds or other obvious "sky" elements.

The prototype for "Peaceful Mountains" features a beautiful sky fabric by Hi-Fashion Fabrics.

Home Dec Fabric

Using a fabric from your home as a starting point for a landscape is a great way to set your home décor apart from the crowd. I have a lot of fun creating a landscape with decorator fabrics that have been used in a room. Maybe that's because I enjoy coordinating all the elements of the room design—the wallpaper, window treatments, furniture, accessories, etc. More than likely you have used several different fabrics in the window treatments, furniture, and pillow accents in a room. These are all possibilities for the point of origin for a landscape.

Designing a landscape from the fabrics in a room is a lovely way to tie all the decorating elements together and create something exciting and unique for the room. It is very unusual to see a wall hanging constructed from the fabrics used in the décor of a room. I am sure you are well aware of the cost of buying artwork for your walls. Making a landscape is a great way to make something beautiful for your home and save money at the same time.

"Tropical Paradise" on page 16 incorporates the fabrics I used to decorate the master bedroom of our home. The collection of fabrics for this room has a base fabric plus several companion pieces. All these fabrics are merged into the landscape design with the exception of one—the bold mauve stripe fabric. Since I cut out a section of the stripes from the base fabric, I chose not to use the additional stripes from one of the companion fabrics. When I am working with a large scale print like the stripe, I look for shapes or color sections from the base fabric to work into the landscape. You just have to be brave, dive in, and start cutting out pieces.

These are the fabrics I used in the bedroom. They work beautifully in the landscape quilt too.

I arrange the pieces at random and reposition them several times before I come up with an arrangement I am comfortable with for the landscape.

"Tropical Paradise" is a wonderful focal point for for our master bedroom. Look at how much extra life and pizzazz it adds to the décor of the bedroom. The wall quilt does a great job of complementing the bedspread, window treatments, tablecloth, lamps, and the pillow accents on the bed. The lampshade is covered with the small floral companion fabric and the base of the lamp is painted with the same paint that is on the wall. There is so much you can do with fabric to decorate your home. I really enjoyed sewing the items in this room and it was fun to add the landscape as the "grand finale."

For "Tropical Paradise" the bedspread fabric was the basis for setting the color theme of the landscape. When using decorator fabrics as a base, the process for selecting companion fabrics gets a little more complicated because there may be several decorator fabrics involved. However, the base fabric is usually the first one chosen, followed by the companion accent fabrics. The base fabric will be representative of the companion fabrics as well. Once you've chosen the base decorator fabric, choose fabrics for the sky, midground, and foreground that will work with it. Keep in mind that you want to incorporate the companion fabrics (pillows, window treatments, etc.) into your landscape design. Now you can finish pulling in the balance of your fabrics with additional pieces that will blend with the base, sky, midground, and foreground fabrics.

The base fabric was incorporated into "Tropical Paradise" in the upper mountains and also

I created "Tropical Paradise" specifically for my master bedroom.

as a floral appliqué on the lower right corner. Sections of the base fabric were cut into shapes for the mountains—the most obvious is the mauve and burgundy striped mountain three layers down from the top. There are three sections of this stripe going across this area in the mountains. Several purple mountain peaks were carved out of the base fabric and many other mountain sections were trimmed out of the base fabric that are light gold and shades of green. I incorporated the base fabric into the mountains by using cuttings that represented all of the colors from the base. The floral print base fabric was perfect for cutting out a few sections of the flowers to be used as appliqués on the lower right corner. These flowers also create close-up detail.

You can see that the bed coverings, pillows, and the wall hanging are made with the same fabrics.

I started the process of cutting out the mountains by first analyzing and identifying the color sections of the base fabric. Then I began trimming around the sections of color and forming them into various mountain shapes. Once I had an assortment of many mountain sections to choose from, I layered them into a design I liked. Since the base fabric is so busy, it needs some other subtle fabrics incorporated with it to give the eye some rest. I call these subtle fabrics "blenders"—very basic fabrics without much design that are chosen from fabrics similar in color to the base fabric.

Here is a view of the master bedroom showing how all the fabrics are incorporated into the landscape and the decorating accents.

Wallpaper

Occasionally the wallpaper in the room can set the theme for the room design and thus become the point of origin for the landscape. In some instances, there may not be a fabric used in the room for the window treatments or pillow accents. In this case, the wallpaper is the key player but it is not a fabric that is utilized in the landscape. It has simply set the stage for the color scheme of the room and the wall hanging. Again, you should start creating the landscape by finding the fabrics for the sky, midground, and the foreground that will work with the colors and mood of the wallpaper.

My "Springtime" landscape is constructed using mostly flower and leaf decorative stitches to go with the wallpaper in the room. There is a large floral wallpaper border that goes around the ceiling on three of the soft creamy yellow walls. The wallpaper on the fireplace wall is a yellow and white stripe with floral vines trailing down. I wanted the landscape to have a feeling of spring and freshness and to reflect the cheerfulness that the wallpaper brings to the décor.

Since we rarely used our living room, we converted it into a sewing room. I get a lot of pleasure from the beauty of the windows in this room and I didn't want to take away from them with window treatments, so I chose to use only pleated shades for the windows. This makes a lovely and inviting sewing room because of the light from the windows.

The colors in "Springtime" coordinate with the wallpaper.

We converted our living room into a sewing room to make better use of the space. I love sewing in this room because of all the windows.

The pastel colors and stitches in this landscape wall hanging were chosen to complement the wallpaper around the fireplace in my sewing room (formerly a little-used living room).

Furniture

Another possible point of origin is furniture. When my daughter asked me to make a landscape for her living room, I could easily see that her beautiful plaid sofa was the focal point in the room. The room had no other objects or window treatments I could pull colors from so the sofa became the basis for designing the landscape. The plaid fabric in the sofa is light blue, dark blue, and white. The floral throw pillows introduce mauve, green, and a soft yellow tone. Plaids and stripes can be tricky to work with, and this was quite a design challenge for me. I began by collecting some checked fabrics in colors I thought would mimic the sofa. Once I found them, I looked for fabrics for the basic three—sky, midground, and foreground.

You can see that the sky fabric I chose for this landscape is perfect with the colors in the sofa. I tucked in the checked fabric mimicking the sofa in three different places. There is a large mountain section near the top, a checkered embroidered house, and some little checked rocks next to the water on the lower

This sofa is so striking, it's obviously the focal point of the room and so became the basis for color selection for the landscape.

The floral throw pillows allowed me to introduce mauve, green, and tan into the landscape.

right. I introduced just a hint of soft yellow to coordinate with the subdued yellow in the accent pillows. The yellow also comes into play in the hot air balloon, sailboat, and the flowers in the lower left corner. Last but not least, the landscape was enhanced with a blue frame and blue and white matting to go with the sofa.

Tricia's landscape coordinates beautifully with her sofa and accent pillows.

Frame

How about designing a landscape using the color of the frame as the point of origin? Pictured on pages 23 and 24 are two landscapes I created especially for the Madeira Thread Company's trade show exhibit. Madeira wanted to frame the landscapes in hunter green, their corporate color, if possible. Fortunately, hunter green is an easy color to build around because it is representative of nature. I thought Madeira's display would be more attractive if I could somehow create a balance by tying the two landscapes together as a pair. I decided to use the same fabric in two different colors for the sky, thereby creating a similar look but two totally different scenes.

In this case, the hunter green is the point of origin, with both sky fabrics having varying tints and shades of that color. However, each sky fabric dictates a very different direction for take-off because of the drastic differences in the colors. The two fabrics used for the skies work very well together even though they aren't fabrics you would normally think of as sky fabrics.

"Blue Midnight" has very deep and dark tones in the sky so I decided to keep the whole landscape fairly dark because it looked like a night sky. One caution though: If the landscape is dark from top to bottom, it can become too deep. It needs a focal point and that's why I made the sails of the boat white, also picking up the whitecaps in the water.

"Just Horsin' Around" was a fun landscape to design because it combines a very unusual grouping of colors. Who would have thought of throwing burgundy in the foreground with the sky and water fabrics that were selected for this landscape? These fabrics work well together because the background fabric for the horses incorporates the same colors found in the sky and water fabrics.

It was really hard for me to give these landscapes up when it came time to ship them to Madeira. Sometimes you become attached to the items you make!

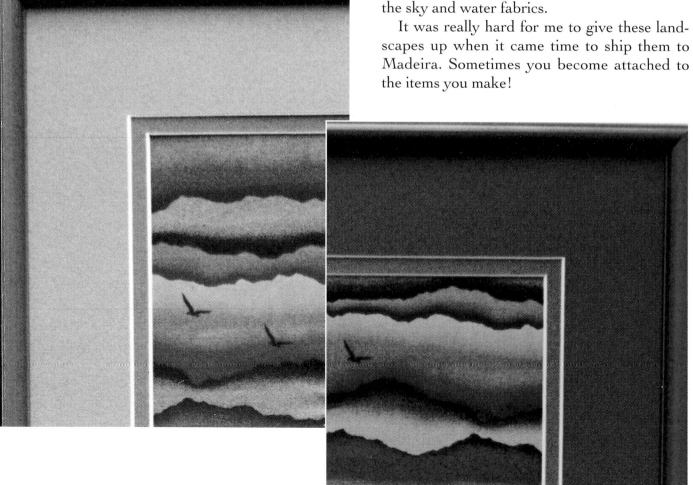

"Blue Midnight."

"Just Horsin' Around."

Summary

When you are looking at fabrics for landscapes, learn to think "outside the box" and expand your horizons. Many fabrics have a lot of potential if you can learn to see them from a completely different perspective.

I have given you just a few examples of points of origin. I am sure you will discover many others. I am confident, however, that you will have a great running start from studying these examples.

Just remember that the three most crucial areas of the landscape are the sky, midground, and foreground. These three fabrics must work well together and have some colors in common to tie everything together. Once you have chosen the three basics, the other pieces of fabric will naturally fall into place. Just dive in and go for it.

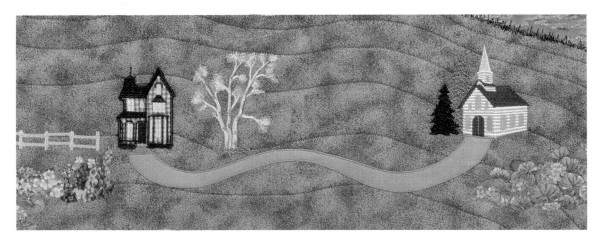

Chapter 3

Making a Pattern

How to Make a Pattern

When making a landscape pattern, the method I use most frequently is to simply make pencil sketches on paper. Any kind of paper will suffice for this purpose. I usually start with a small sketch and if I like what I see, I enlarge the sketch to the size of landscape I have in mind. From the sketch, I can redraw it to a larger size on a bigger piece of paper (or you can quickly enlarge a sketch on a copy machine by increasing the copy size).

Another method I use is a dry erase board and markers. This is much faster than using a pencil and paper and you can quickly erase and sketch out a design. After I have drawn something I like, I can lay a piece of pattern tracing paper over the board and trace the sketch for the pattern.

If you have a photo or postcard you'd like to use as the basis for a fabric landscape, use a copy machine to enlarge the original to landscape size. Then make a pattern by laying a piece of tracing paper or waxed paper over the landscape and tracing the shapes. Keep in mind that the landscape picture belongs to the artist. You may make a fabric landscape for yourself, but you cannot sell the landscape. Always give credit to the artist on a label that you place on your landscape.

The "River Bend" pattern shown below originated from a landscape I found in computer clip art. I enlarged the landscape design on the copy machine several times until it was the size I wanted. Then I traced the elements of the landscape and made the pattern. I changed some of the lines of the landscape slightly to make it more interesting or easier to maneuver around the curves when sewing with the decorative stitches on the machine.

"River Bend" was adapted from computer clip art. Clip art is a wonderful source for landscape designs, as are postcards, calendars, and paintings.

This is the clip art I modified for the "River Bend" pattern. The lines of this landscape are easily identifiable, which makes it a wonderful subject for a pattern.

I have used my patterns over again many times to create new landscapes. It is amazing how the same pattern can look so different when you change the fabrics. You can also change the look of the landscape with different embellishments. I have chosen two landscapes constructed with the "Sail Away" pattern (page 80) to demonstrate what I mean. These two landscapes are identical from the pattern standpoint, but made with different fabrics and embellishments.

Many of the landscapes pictured in this book are created from the "Peaceful Mountains" pattern (pattern #104, Linda Crone Creations). You can use the patterns in this book to make an endless variety of landscapes without ever making two that look exactly alike. Or use the patterns in the book as a launching pad to create your own variations.

The fabrics in this landscape are bold primary colors, making it very vibrant. A machine embroidered sailboat from the same color family is the final touch.

The cool colored fabrics give the landscape a quieter look. The machine embroidered tree accented with rhinestones and rock beads create a unique accent.

Designing Without a Pattern

I also enjoy creating landscapes without a pattern. I call this the "design as you go" method. It's fun to just start rotary cutting some curves from an assortment of fabrics and see what you can do with them. I start by layering the cut pieces together in an arrangement until I come up with a design I visually like. I usually rearrange them several times. "Springtime," the landscape in my sewing room, was created using this method. I pulled together a collection of soft pastel fabrics that I wanted to use in the landscape. I began by randomly cutting the strips of fabric with the rotary cutter, creating the mountain shapes for the top five mountains. I arranged them in several different configurations until I kept coming back to a design I liked best. I asked myself which fabric looked best next to the sky, which fabric contrasted with the water, which colors worked side-by-side, and which should be separated by another color of fabric between them. I

had saved the fabric with the large scale blue flowers for the close-up detail placed in the foreground.

Consider turning your fabric pieces over and check to see if the backside has any possibilities. Keep the scraps that you trimmed away. Maybe the reverse side of the curve you threw aside has potential too.

Another method I use for designing without a pattern is to sketch out the pieces one by one. Start by cutting out the first shape, a mountain for example. Then lay a piece of pattern tracing paper or waxed paper over the first piece and sketch the second piece. Cut the second landscape piece out by using the pattern you just traced. Repeat this process for the rest of the landscape.

Newspaper is handy for cutting out different shapes to experiment with as you design. It helps you visualize what a piece will look like in fabric. It is easy to adjust the size and placement with newspaper and it helps prevent wasted fabric.

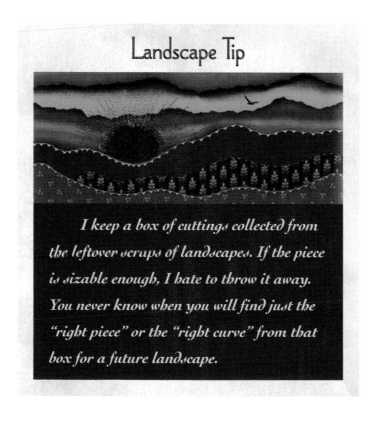

Landscape Tip

I keep a box of cuttings collected from the leftover scraps of landscapes. If the piece is sizable enough, I hate to throw it away. You never know when you will find just the "right piece" or the "right curve" from that box for a future landscape.

"Springtime" was a fun and relaxing landscape to design by using my "design as you go" method. It's easy—just relax, play, and cut a few rotary curves!

Getting Started

$a$lthough the focus of this book features land-scapes constructed with decorative stitches, there are many beautiful scenes that can be produced with a few basic stitches or even just the zigzag stitch. Many techniques illustrated in this book can be achieved with any basic sewing machine.

Proper Sewing Machine Feet

These feet are designed just for decorative stitches with the wide grooves on the bottom of the foot.

If you are using decorative stitches, your machine manual will tell you which feet are appropriate to use. These feet usually have a wide channel or groove on the underside that allows for the buildup of thread to easily pass under the foot as you sew. Some decorative stitches are more thread intensive, so using the right foot is critical to the beauty of the stitch.

The **walking foot** (also called the even-feed foot or dual feed) comes in handy for some stages of the construction process, especially if you are going to bind the landscape as a wall hanging or utilize it on a garment. This foot helps feed the layers of fabric evenly from the top and bottom. Walking feet are available for most machines. Use the walking foot designed for your machine or find a generic one that works on your machine. Check with your sewing machine dealer if you need help with this selection.

For some of the sewing techniques, such as creating grass, outlining around flowers, or thread painting, I like to use **free-motion stitching**. In free-motion stitching, the feed dogs on the machine are lowered and you move the fabric around yourself. If your machine doesn't have this feature, you can simply put a piece of tape over the feed dogs. There are a number of different feet you can use to free-motion stitch. Your machine probably came with a darning foot, which can easily be used for this purpose. I prefer to use just the bare needle because that allows me a better view of the fabric. Just don't forget to lower the presser foot in this instance. It's easy to forget to do that when there's no foot there as a visual reminder.

I occasionally use the fringe foot to create grass—an easy embellishing technique with this foot. Set the stitch width at 3.0—just wide enough to hop over the center bar in the middle of the foot on both sides. Set the stitch length at 0.5. The grass will be thicker and fuller by using a short stitch length. You may want to run two threads through the needle at the same time for more fullness in the grass. I like to stitch several rows of loops, stabilize them from the backside, then cut the loops to fluff up the grass. See Chapter 8 on embellishing techniques for more detail about this method.

The grass in the photo was stitched with bright red thread so you can easily see how the fringe is formed. Of course, you probably wouldn't normally stitch grass with red thread!

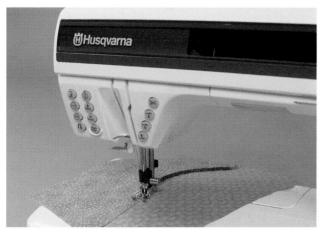

The fringe foot creates large loops as it swings over the bar in the center with a zigzag stitch. You can see the loops coming off the back of the foot.

Landscape Tip

By experimenting, I've found that it is important to use a foot that doesn't separate or open in the middle. The regular feet used for straight stitching and zigzag often do. When you use a foot that separates in the middle, it encourages the fabric to scoot or feed up between the toes of the foot where it opens. This causes wrinkles or puckers and the landscape will not lay flat. The foot needs to ride on top of the raw edge, holding the fabric nice and flat as you sew over it. The photo shows how the foot should be positioned on the fabric.

The open-toed appliqué foot causes the same problem, so avoid using it too. This was a real surprise to me. I have tried using the open-toe foot on several different occasions with the same poor results.

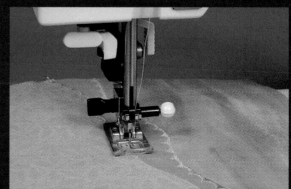

This foot rides perfectly on top of the fabric, holding it in a good position for decorative stitches. It also separates to the far left side, which will not cause puckering.

Needles

Selecting the right needle for the task is an important step in sewing a successful project. Each time you start a new project, start with a new needle. It is best to have an assortment of needles on hand so you are fully equipped to do the job. There is no limit to the variety of threads you will be using, so you will need several different types of needles.

The needles I use most frequently for landscape construction are embroidery, metallic, and topstitch needles. This chart will give you helpful information for needles and threads. The "flat films" are threads such as Sulky Sliver, Madeira Jewel, or Superior Glitter to name a few.

Needle & Sizes	Description	Threads	Stitches
Embroidery 80/12–90/14	Larger eye prevents fraying of threads	Rayon Flat films	Decorative Straight Machine Embroidery
Metallic 80/12–90/14	Larger eye prevents fraying of threads	Metallic Flat films	Decorative Straight Machine Embroidery
Topstitch 80/12–100/20	Extra large eye for heavier threads	Heavy or textured	Decorative Straight Two threads through the needle
Twin Embroidery 2.0/75–3.0/75	Larger eye prevents fraying of threads	Rayon Flat films	Decorative Straight
Twin Metallic 2.0/80–3.0/80	Larger eye prevents fraying of threads	Metallic Flat films	Decorative Straight

Supplies

You probably have most of the basic sewing supplies you will need to do landscapes — pencil, fusible web, scissors, pins, ruler, rotary cutter and mat, and pattern tracing paper. Beyond these basics, the following products will save you time and effort.

These are some of the notions that are so helpful. Quiltgard (fabric protector), 505 (temporary positioning adhesive), Sulky KK 2000 (temporary spray adhesive), Sulky stabilizers, HeatnBond Lite (iron-on adhesive web), Madeira Avalon (plastic type stabilizer), and large circle template by Staedtler.

Stabilizers

Stabilizers are a must-have item when working with decorative stitches and machine embroidery. Stabilizers support the stitches and fabric and help prevent distortion, puckering, tunneling, and skipped stitches. There is a great assortment of stabilizers to choose from in many different forms. Some are woven or nonwoven fabric, paper, and plastic. I like to keep some of each on hand so I'm always ready to tackle any project.

I like to use a stabilizer with firm support for the decorative stitches and machine embroidery. These include Stitch-N-Tear by Pellon, Sulky Tear-Easy Stabilizer, or Husqvarna Tear-A-Way Stabilizer. It's important to choose a stabilizer that won't distort the stitches when you remove it. I use the plastic-like stabilizers to create machine embroidery flowers for appliqué. My favorites are Madeira Avalon, Husqvarna Dissolve-A-Way, and Sulky Solvy.

Muslin

In almost all my landscapes, I use a piece of muslin as the foundation fabric for the landscape construction. I always use it for garments. If the landscape is going to be in a picture frame or greeting card, it can be constructed directly on top of a piece of stabilizer. Many times when I start sewing a landscape I don't know how it will be used. When in doubt, always start with the muslin because it has more versatility than stabilizers.

I use muslin because I don't want to use a foundation fabric that might shadow through the landscape pieces. You may use a scrap of fabric instead of muslin for the base, but be sure it won't shadow through behind the landscape fabrics. The base fabric can be any light colored solid fabric. If your landscape is composed of mostly dark fabrics, you can use a dark colored solid fabric as a base.

Temporary Spray Adhesives

I highly recommend using temporary spray adhesives for the construction process. These adhesives take the place of using pins. They are adhesives that don't bond permanently and the bonding agent disappears in two to five days. Temporary spray adhesives help hold the landscape in place during the stitching process, and thereby improve the quality of the stitches and prevent puckers. The fabric can't scoot as easily under the sewing machine foot as it can when you use pins alone.

Most spray adhesives allow you to reposition your fabric if necessary. There are many readily available temporary adhesives such as Sulky KK 2000, 505 by Odif, and Sullivans.

Fabric Protector

A fabric protector does just what the name implies—protects fabric. I like to use a product called Quiltgard to protect my finished landscapes from liquids, soil, and grease. It comes in an aerosol can and is sprayed on the fabric. If you have spent many hours lovingly creating something, consider using fabric protector to help preserve your creative endeavors. Fabric protector won't change the texture or the color of the fabric, it simply coats the fabric with a liquid repellent, which helps reduce fading as well.

I recommend treating your finished landscapes with a fabric protector. It's inexpensive and can save your masterpiece from damage.

Millimeter Ruler

A millimeter ruler is a handy little tool I use quite frequently. Most of the designs on software embroidery cards give the design measurement in millimeters. When I am incorporating an embroidery design in a landscape, it is very helpful to be able to measure exactly how the design will fit. You can purchase one of these at an office supply store or in the sewing notions department at a fabric store.

Circle Template

Here is another great gadget I use often. It is a template of many different size circles. I use it to determine how large I want to make the sun/moon in a landscape design. You can trace the size of the circle you need from the template right onto your fabric. You should be able to find a circle template at an office supply store or fabric store.

Free-Motion Stitching Aids

There are many tools available for free-motion stitching. A couple of my favorites are rubber fingertips and a pair of garden or quilter's gloves with the small rubber dots on the fingers and palms. They help you grip and maneuver the fabric easily through the machine. I find that wearing the gloves or rubber fingertips helps me relax when I am doing free-motion embroidery.

Another helpful tool is a flexible hoop called Quilt Sew Easy. It has handles on the sides, cushions on the bottom to grip the fabric, and you may pick it up to easily reposition while free-motion stitching. I don't use the traditional wooden or plastic hoops for hooping the fabric because the work space inside the hoop is too confining. You may want to try several different approaches until you find what suits you best.

Sewing Table Extension

This book features landscapes in all shapes and sizes. When you are constructing a landscape bigger than 8" x 10", the landscape becomes somewhat difficult to handle. To make the job easier, I suggest that you use a plexiglass portable sewing table to extend the work surface of your machine. These units are designed to wrap around the free arm of the sewing machine. Check with your sewing machine dealer for a brand specific item. The table extension makes the whole construction process much easier.

The Design Concepts

When I took one of my landscapes to be framed recently, the woman who worked at the shop studied the scene and said, "This just makes you want to go there, to wherever that magical place is." When she said that, it gave me goose bumps! I didn't realize a picture of mine could have that kind of impact on someone. She really loved that landscape. A big smile came across her face and her eyes lit up with fascination and interest. This is what I want to achieve in this chapter: I want you to understand the design concepts and to be able to create something wonderful that will be an inspiration to someone else.

In this chapter, I outline some general guidelines regarding the design process. There is no right or wrong, only general principles for designing. As they say, "Rules are made to be broken," and sometimes I do the very opposite of what I have suggested. The artist in you has the freedom to do what you like. That's what transforms creativity into art.

When I am designing, I try to listen to my inner voice. Certain thoughts come to me as I work with fabrics. "Yes, I like this. It looks great." Or, "Something doesn't feel right here. What is it?" I find that my gut instincts are usually right, and that I should listen to them more often. Most of us need to trust our inner voice to improve our skills as an artist. If I am having trouble making decisions about which fabrics to use, I know I am too tired and it is time to walk away for a while. The next day, when I am rested, I find I can quickly make the decisions I struggled with yesterday. It's amazing what a little rest or a good night's sleep will do for you.

Chapter 2, The Design Process, addressed the point of origin and where the planning process could begin. This chapter offers a more detailed look at planning and pulling your fabrics together.

I have devised my own system for how to arrange fabrics together. I am not suggesting that this is the only right way to do it, but it seems comfortable and works well for me. You may find another approach you like better. As I mentioned earlier, these are only guidelines.

Choosing the First Three Fabrics

First find three fabrics that work well together for the sky, middle ground, and foreground.

The first thing I do is choose three fabrics that work well together for the sky, middle ground, and foreground. Your landscape will have greater continuity and will be more appealing to the eye if these three fabrics have some colors in common. This helps them appear more connected, tied together, or have a "visual balance." In the photo on page 35 you can see how the fabrics for the sky, middle ground, and foreground work together. The three fabrics have blues and greens in common. It would be very easy to start building a landscape around these fabrics because they are so well connected.

scale than the houses you see in the distance. This is a good example of close-up detail. You can see the detail of the cats sitting in the windows, where you can only see an image of the windows in the distant houses. The red poppies are a real attention grabber and a good example of color placement. They need to be positioned somewhere in the foreground because they are so brilliant in color and they will bounce forward as the eye views this landscape. The red poppies are positioned behind the large yellow daisies in the foreground because they are smaller in size than the largest yellow daisies in the foreground.

Creating Depth

Another basic design principle is creating a feeling of depth. If I were standing on the foreground of the landscape, the view in the distance would diminish and appear farther away. What is closer to me should be clearer, more distinct in detail, and larger in scale. This principle is evident when the trees in the foreground are larger than the trees in the distance. Depth can be developed in a number of ways such as through the use of color placement, scale of fabric, texture, lines, and close-up detail.

There are many lessons about depth in "Florals of Provence." Scale of fabric is demonstrated through the placement of the different sizes of the flowers. The largest flowers are placed in the front or foreground and the smallest are in the more distant background. The flowers graduate in scale from the largest, to the middle sized, and then to the smallest. The brown house in the foreground is much larger in

The "Florals of Provence" landscape has a very realistic feeling of depth.

Fabric As a Design Element

One of the best things about designing landscapes with fabric is that it takes so little fabric. You probably already have a good assortment of fabrics in your stash of scraps. A little bit goes a long way—1/8 to 1/4 yard is plenty to work with in most cases. However, it seems that no matter how much fabric we have at home, we never have just the right piece! For those of us who are very tuned into color, that is both a blessing and a curse. There's nothing better than another excuse to go to the fabric store! I often buy a little piece of this and a little piece of that—a piece of cotton, tissue lamé, blouse fabric, netting, corduroy, etc. What I am really looking for is color, texture, and different size prints. The store clerks at the cutting table frequently ask me what I'm making because they can't see any relationship between the little bits and pieces of fabric I purchase. When I tell them I'm making a landscape, I often get a funny look. I know they think I'm out of my mind—it's so obvious on their faces!

I literally use any type of fabric in my landscapes including cottons (of course), or silk, polyester, knit, leather, suede, or whatever you can imagine. Using a variety of fabrics helps create interest. Some fabrics should be fused with a fusible interfacing on the backside to stabilize them for landscape construction. Stretchy fabrics like knits, or perhaps sueded rayon which is very slippery, will handle much better when they are stabilized. If the landscape is going to be either hand or machine washed, you must take this into consideration when you are choosing your fabrics. Obviously, some fabrics are not meant to be washed, and dry cleaning is the preferred method for cleaning.

Pay attention to the scale of the fabric—the size of the print. As a general rule, the larger the print, the closer it should be to the foreground or at the bottom of the landscape. The opposite is true for smaller prints—they should be placed further back in the distance of your scene. Arrange all the fabrics on the table from the smallest print up to the largest in scale. As you begin the placement of the prints, you will quickly recognize where the best position is according to their scale.

Be careful with prints, plaids, and stripes. Your landscape can get too busy in a hurry if too many of these are included in one scene. If the scale of the print is quite small, you might get by with using one or more print. Again, it comes down to a personal preference and what is pleasing to your eye. To maintain harmony in the overall look and feel of the landscape, there should be a visual balance in the selection of fabrics.

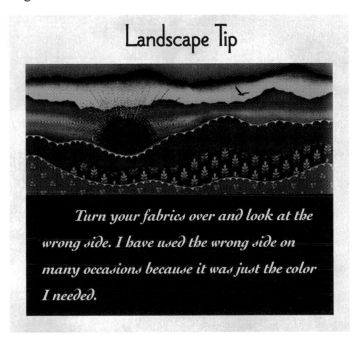

Landscape Tip

Turn your fabrics over and look at the wrong side. I have used the wrong side on many occasions because it was just the color I needed.

Shading Fabrics

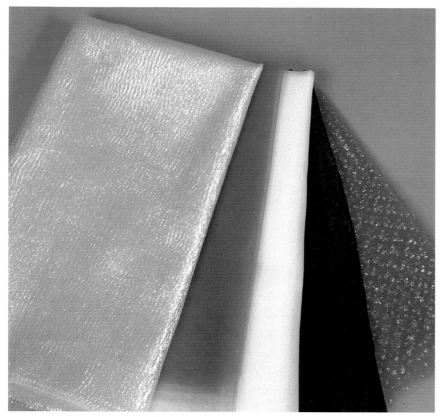

To soften a color, I sometimes layer a sheer fabric over another fabric.

Look through all the departments, including the drapery and formal wear sections. Sometimes we get into a rut and have trouble thinking outside the box. I challenge you to look at fabrics from a completely different perspective and see the possibilities for sky, water, land, trees, and so forth. For example, there are lots of interesting fabrics besides cotton that would make magnificent water—tissue lamé, satin, moiré, foiled knits, sequined knits, or crinkled organza are a few examples.

Some lightweight fabrics are difficult to work with because they have a tendency to shift. You can eliminate this problem by fusing lightweight interfacing on the back of the fabric to stabilize it and make it much easier to handle.

On some occasions, I like to layer a sheer fabric over another fabric to shade it to another color. Sheer netting and organza fabrics are wonderful for this technique. I keep a collection of sheer fabrics on hand just for this purpose. In many cases, they are so subtle you can barely see them.

Water Fabrics

The beauty of creating landscapes is that "anything goes" as far as the choice of fabrics are concerned. Any fabric in your stash or in the store is a candidate for a landscape. I find most of my fabrics at the local chain fabric stores and quilt shops.

When looking for water fabrics, don't limit yourself to cotton. Try lamé, foiled knit, crinkled organza, or some other "interesting" choice.

Blending Fabrics

Blending fabrics play a very important role in merging all the colors and prints together. These fabrics give the eye some rest. They are generally solid or very small print and are more subtle or muted in appearance than the dominant fabrics. Examples of blenders are batiks, hand dyes, or mottled fabrics where the colors fade in and out. When placed between two strong prints, blender fabrics help make the transition.

I'm not comfortable placing too many print fabrics adjacent to each other. The overall look starts to get too busy for me. I much prefer a landscape that is balanced with blenders and prints.

Blender fabrics are subtle or muted and help balance strong prints.

Marrying Fabrics

Marrying fabrics introduce a new color into the palette. For a good example of how marrying fabrics work, look at "Just Horsin' Around" below.

The three most important fabrics in this landscape (sky, midground, and foreground) have similar tones of green in common. However, the horse fabric in the foreground introduces a new color—burgundy. If you were to analyze just the sky and water fabrics, you probably wouldn't consider adding burgundy to the mix. Because some of the horses are burgundy, using this fabric allows the addition of other fabrics with burgundy. The marrying fabric could be almost any of the pieces in the landscape. In this case, it's the horse print in the foreground.

The horse fabric in the foreground introduces burgundy into the landscape and "marries" other fabrics with burgundy tones.

Texture

A number of fabrics have texture—burlap, corduroy, velvet, suede, fleece, or crinkled fabric. The main thing to keep in mind is that texture should be placed on or near the foreground if you want it to grab your attention. Try to keep it in direct relationship to the size of the landscape. In other words, I wouldn't use a piece of fleece in a greeting-card-size landscape, but it might work well in a much larger variation. Since we are always trying to create depth, a dominant texture should be near the foreground.

The tree looks so real in this picture, I feel like I could reach out and touch it. Patsy Shields, who is an educator with Sulky of America, used fabric that has been crinkled to create the tree and part of the foreground. Crinkling is an easy procedure where you wet the fabric, twist it up in a ball, and let it dry. Once dry, you stretch it out like an accordion and secure the wrinkles in place by fusing a fusible interfacing on the backside of the fabric. (See the book *Creating Texture with Textiles* by Linda McGehee for more information on crinkling.)

Textured fabrics such as a crinkled fabric or wide wale corduroy need to be placed in or near the foreground because they will visually come forward. These fabrics help create a sense of depth when they are positioned properly in a landscape.

The textured tree and foreground (left front) were created from crinkled fabrics, giving the foreground a three-dimensional look.

Lines As a Design Element

You will notice that most of my landscapes have gentle curving lines. The pieces are cut and sewn with these gentle lines for two reasons. First, I like the landscape to have a calming effect, and gentle curving lines help achieve that. The repetition of the curving lines also helps create a rhythm. Second, since I like to use decorative stitches for the construction process, it is much easier to stitch around curves than it is to stitch around jagged edges. Horizontal lines have a calming effect, while vertical lines tend to create more excitement. It seems to me that we have plenty of excitement in this world, and most of us could use a dose of something that calms us down once in a while!

Creating Depth With Lines

Using wider layers of lines or bigger pieces in the foreground will make the background seem more distant.

The lines of a landscape (design of the pattern) come into play when trying to create depth. The size of the sections of the land or objects in the foreground should be larger than the size of the land and objects in the distance. You can also create more depth by adding close-up detail in the foreground that looks as realistic as if you were standing right there looking at it. The flowers, trees, and plants in the foreground of "Tropical Paradise" were created to give you that feeling.

Another example of close-up detail is shown in the photo on page 43. The large tree in the foreground, combined with the grass and rock beads, shows scale when compared with the snow-capped mountain in the background. The tree not only creates depth, but also helps develop a three-dimensional look.

The large foreground sections of land in "Tropical Paradise" help make the mountains in the background appear more distant.

Placing a large and detailed element in the foreground creates depth.

Color As a Design Element

Color is such an intriguing subject, I really get excited about it. I believe people overwhelmingly underestimate its power and impact. You've heard that "Love makes the world go around," but I believe that color makes the world go around. Many of us don't fully comprehend the relationship color has to our everyday lives and our emotions. It's interesting to note that studies have shown that houses sell or don't sell based on color alone.

Color creates a mood. It has a temperature and it says a lot about you. Color can be striking, tranquil, exciting, dull, warm, cold, feminine, or masculine. When you begin designing anything, but especially landscapes, give color careful consideration, because it has much more impact than we give it credit for.

We know that the warm colors such as yellow, orange, and red "advance." If you use these colors in a landscape, they will move visually forward toward you. Use them in an area where you want to accentuate a detail or perhaps in the foreground area if you want to make the background more distant.

Cool colors such as blue, purple, and green "recede." That means they will move back visually as you view the landscape. Use these colors in areas where you need to create more depth, such as the background in the distance or in a detail that you want to be subtle. Learn to use the colors to your advantage in creating realistic landscapes.

Here's a brief summary of what some colors symbolize.

Red—passionate, associated with romance, symbolizes the pulse of life, attracts attention, actually speeds up the body's metabolism, and says, "look at me." Red advances visually.

Yellow—lively, happy, joyful, the color of sunshine and daffodils. Yellow is the lightest and brightest color in the color wheel. A little bit goes a long way and it advances forward quickly.

Orange—stimulates the appetite, the color of many foods (oranges, cantaloupes, apricots, peaches, carrots, squash), the color of fall. Orange evokes strong emotion, a color that is much disliked, advances visually forward.

Blue—cool, restful, calming, young, sporty, reduces blood pressure, has many moods depending on its shade, the color of the sky and sea, the easiest color for most people to wear, visually recedes.

Green—symbolizes nature, trees, grass, an easy color to be around, brings balance to other colors. Bright greens can represent spring, mildew, even poison and jealousy. Green can be both warm and cool. It bridges the gap between blue and yellow on the color wheel. Yellow greens are considered warm and tend to advance, where blue greens are cool and will recede.

Purple—associated with royalty, sophisticated, rare in nature, evokes elements of magic and surprise, can be bold as in bright purple or soft as in lavender. Visually recedes.

In designing landscapes, we need a good understanding of what happens with color in relationship to its placement. Warm colors advance and cool colors recede, so if you are trying to create depth, use colors in the distant background that are going to recede. In that case, you would probably use blues, grays, and soft greens. The foreground is a good place to position warm colors such as red, orange, or yellow because they advance visually.

Occasionally, you might want to put a streak of bright color somewhere in the landscape to create some excitement. In quilting terminology they call this a "zinger." I am careful not to overuse zingers because I don't want them to become the main focal point.

What about light vs. dark colors? Which ones recede and which ones advance? The answer is that it can be either because it depends on the background. I have read several conflicting opinions about this, so I consulted a respected local artist, Tom Heflin. Tom was very helpful and gave me a couple examples. "If it is dark outside and a man comes walking up the street in a white suit, then the man in white advances. If it is daylight and you look outside and see a dark tree, then the tree advances." In other words, if a dark color is surrounded by light colors, the dark color will advance. And if a light color is surrounded by dark colors, then the light color will advance.

The easiest way to improve your design skills is to better understand color. Sometimes we tend to hurry through things and don't take time to study, think, and devise a great plan for a project. With landscapes, it is important to use all the tools in the toolbox, especially the colors.

Naturally, we have a tendency to use colors that are our favorites and exclude the rest. We decorate our homes with the same colors we enjoy wearing. Believe it or not, we have developed color prejudices that are usually emotion-

ally attached to some event or person of the past. These feelings about color can either be pleasant memories or bad ones. It is interesting to hear what associations people have to color regarding past experiences. As for myself, I always associate the color pink with my grandmother. She loved pink, chose it frequently for many things, and was happy to tell you she loved pink. I have a very warm feeling for that color because my grandmother was very kind, loving, quiet, and never said a bad word about anyone. On the other hand, I have always disliked sage green. It wasn't until a few years ago that I was able to understand why I disliked it so much. I was a shy grade school student and one teacher in particular intimidated me. One day she asked me a question and I didn't answer her because I was afraid I might have the wrong answer. In front of the class she said, "Linda, I am going to take you to see the nurse and get your ears cleaned, because obviously you can't hear." You can imagine how humiliated I felt. I remember sitting in the chair beside the nurse and staring at the wall as she cleaned my ears. Guess what color those walls were? Sage green—forever engraved in my mind and

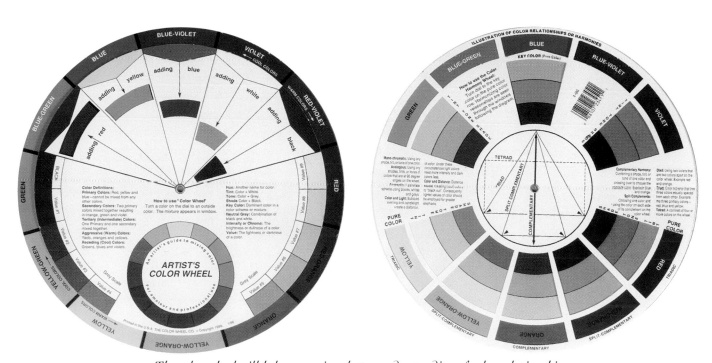

The color wheel will help you gain a better understanding of color relationships.

associated with a very unpleasant moment! I have since given myself permission to use that color. I even painted the walls of our master bedroom sage green!

Whatever negative feelings you have about certain colors, try to get over it. You will be a much better designer by allowing yourself to play with all the colors on the color wheel. Besides, God used all the wonderful colors in the rainbow when he painted this earth.

I enjoy working with the Artist's Color Wheel by The Color Wheel Co. It is a two-sided color wheel that is extremely helpful in the designing process. One side of the wheel shows all the colors around the outside of the wheel and has an inner circle that spins around to show what color you get when you add one of the following colors to it: red, yellow, blue, white, or black. The other side of the color wheel shows what happens to each of the pure colors when you add white, gray, or black to them. This side also has an inner circle that helps identify the colors that are incorporated in the various color schemes. If you don't have a color wheel, I recommend purchasing one. They are inexpensive and easy to use and there is much you can learn by studying one.

There are four scales of color: pure hues, tints, shades, and tones. **Pure hues** are the vibrant pure colors: red, orange, yellow-orange, yellow, yellow-green, green, blue-green, blue, blue-violet, violet, and red-violet. A landscape composed of pure colors will command your attention and be very vibrant. **Tints** are pure colors with white added, creating pastels. Adding white tends to cool down the color, especially the warm ones. Pastels include lavender, pink, peach, powder blue, and mint green. The tint scale is a good choice to reflect spring or a soft and gentle mood. **Shades** are pure colors mixed with black. Shades are always darker than the pure color. Warm shades remind us of autumn and are a great choice for a fall landscape. Warm shades include brown, copper, burnt orange, olive, gold, and pumpkin. Cool shades are a good choice for a night scene. Cool shades include navy, plum, forest green, and maroon. **Tones** are pure colors mixed with gray. Depending on the lightness or darkness of gray, a tone can be lighter, darker, or the same value as the hue. The tone scale is a good choice to convey winter. Tones include slate blue, sage green, heather, rose, and beige.

Take the time to study what happens to colors when they are mixed. It will be very enlightening and will help you make decisions regarding your color choices. Greens in particular can be tricky, and if you recognize whether it is a yellow-green or a blue-green base, it will help you to make better choices regarding the visual balance of your landscape.

Glossary of Color Terms

Achromatic colors: white, black, or a mix of the two. An infinite number of grays can be mixed using white and black.

Adjacent colors: hues next to each other on the color wheel.

Complementary colors: hues opposite each other on the color wheel.

Cool colors: blue, green, violet, and their tints and shades.

Hue: another word for color.

Intensity or saturation: the brightness or dullness of a color.

Intermediate or tertiary colors: one primary and one secondary color mixed together or two secondary colors mixed together.

Primary colors: red, yellow, and blue. The three colors from which all other colors are made.

Secondary colors: green, orange, and violet. Colors created when you mix two primary colors.

Shade: color with black added to it.

Tint: color with white added to it.

Tone: color with gray added to it.

Value: the lightness or darkness of a color.

Warm colors: red, orange, yellow, and their tints and shades.

Color Schemes

A **monochromatic** color scheme uses one color and its tints, shades, and tones. An **analogous** color scheme uses adjacent colors on the color wheel and can include tints, shades, and tones. On the color wheel, an analogous color scheme is any three colors beside each other. These two color schemes are the easiest to work with when you begin designing landscapes. They are very pleasing to the eye and most often restful. Because these two schemes are closely related in color, without as much contrast, the flow of the landscape will come together without as much effort.

A **complementary** color scheme uses two colors opposite each on the color wheel. It can also include tints, shades, and tones. A **split complementary** color scheme uses one color and the two colors on each side of its opposite on the color wheel. A **triad** color scheme uses any three colors equally spaced from each other on the color wheel and a **tetrad** color scheme uses a contrast of four or more colors on the wheel.

I try to balance the colors in my landscapes from the sky down to the bottom of the foreground. For example, if I have used yellow in the background, I will also incorporate yellow into the flowers in the foreground area. The overall appearance of the landscape looks more connected this way.

Taking time to study color in depth is time well spent. It is the quickest way to sharpen your skills and become a better artist with fabric. Once you understand the technical side of color better, you will gain more confidence in working with fabrics. Setting all the technical knowledge aside, it still comes down to a matter of choice and what is most pleasing to your eye.

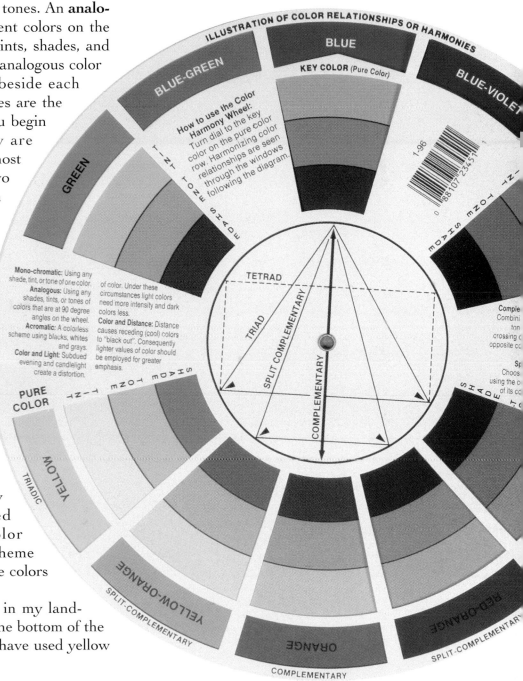

Chapter 6

Decorative Stitches & How to Use Them

i am truly fascinated with all the decorative stitches that sewing machines can do today. Our ancestors would be in total shock if they could see what we have available to us. One focus of my work is finding ways to utilize these fabulous stitch patterns. Landscapes can provide a wonderful palette for you to expand your horizons to use the decorative stitches and create a work of art. Think of the decorative stitches as your paintbrush. What do you want to paint with them?

Styles of Stitches

There are many different styles of stitches and they bring a new life to landscapes. Some stitches are open and airy, while others are more closed and filled in. Stitches are often categorized as utility, practical, embroidery, or decorative in your sewing machine manual.

Open stitches are not completely filled in with thread and may not thoroughly encase the raw edge. **Closed stitches** are filled in more heavily with thread and can finish a raw edge. Of course, there are varying degrees of stitches in both categories. Some of the stitches may encase the raw edges but still be considered open stitches. A zigzag stitch is a good example of a stitch that catches the raw edge but is still an open stitch because it is not filled in with thread. The exception would be when a zigzag stitch is used as a satin stitch with a .5 stitch length, thereby completely finishing the raw edge.

Open Stitches

Light and airy open stitches are the most subtle stitches because they blend with the background. Like the name states, they are less filled in with thread. The majority of the stitches on your stitch menu will probably fall into the open stitch category. Zigzag, feather, appliqué, fagoting, and some overlock stitches are examples of other open stitches. Of course there are many decorative stitches like the ones featured in the photo below that are open stitches as well.

Decorative stitches (leaves, honeycomb, and a stippling stitch) with one thread in the needle. These are light and airy open stitches.

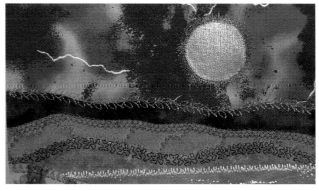

Two threads in the needle. See how adding an additional thread changes the look of the stitches.

An open stitch can be made more visible by using two threads through the needle. The landscape in the bottom photo on page 48 is stitched with the same stitches as the first photo, but I used two threads through the needle. Adding that additional thread makes a big difference in the appearance of the stitches.

Closed Stitches

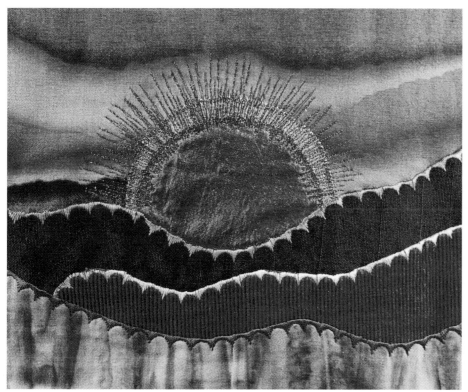

The embroidery satin stitch on the mountain ridges is a closed stitch that adds interesting detail.

a .5 stitch length, it has a very beautiful but simple style all of its own.

Take the time to study the stitches in your sewing machine manual. Try to look at them from a different perspective. What kind of feeling do you want to create? Do you want the landscape to have a very soft, light feeling? If so, use stitches that the eye will move across easily, such as open stitches. If you want your landscape to really make a statement, incorporate more closed stitches that are dynamic and readily visible. Or use a combination of stitches, with open stitches in areas of the landscape you want to be subtle and closed stitches in portions of the landscape you want to accentuate.

Overlock stitches that slant to the left or right can even give the land a feeling of movement. The style of stitches you choose will be a very important part of the mood you create.

All of the stitches can be very helpful in developing depth, which is one of the visual elements you are

Closed stitches tend to be heavier looking. They create more contrast and definition of the land shapes due to the heavy buildup of thread. An example of a closed stitch is the embroidery satin stitch shown in the photo above. It is one of my favorites because it also gives the impression of ridges along the mountain top.

Another example of a closed stitch is a satin zigzag—one of the basic construction stitches. When a zigzag is used as a satin stitch with

The satin zigzag along the ridge tops is simple and beautiful.

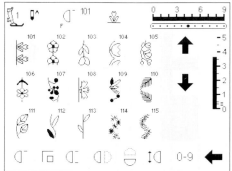

A sampling of open stitches from the Bernina sewing machine manual. Copyright © 1999 Bernina of America, Inc. Reprinted by permission of Bernina of America, Inc.

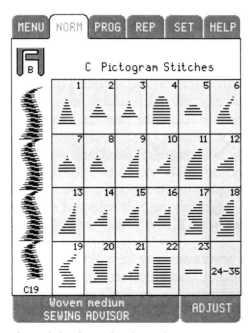

A sampling of closed stitches from the Bernina sewing machine manual. Copyright © 1999 Bernina of America, Inc. Reprinted by permission of Bernina of America, Inc.

A sampling of open stitches from the Husqvarna/Viking sewing machine manual. Reprinted by permission of Husqvarna/Viking.

A sampling of closed stitches from the Husqvarna/Viking sewing machine manual. Reprinted by permission of Husqvarna/Viking.

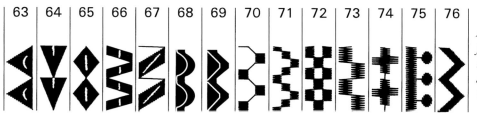

A sampling of closed stitches from the Pfaff sewing machine manual. Reprinted by permission of Pfaff American Sales Corp.

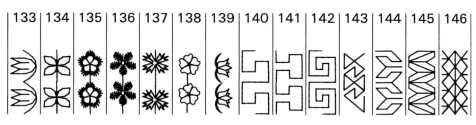

A sampling of open stitches from the Pfaff sewing machine manual. Reprinted by permission of Pfaff American Sales Corp.

always trying to achieve. By adjusting the width of the stitches, you can subtly develop depth. The distant background should have a smaller stitch width such as 5.0 millimeter, then gradually work up to 9 millimeter in the foreground area. If your machine only stitches up to a 6 millimeter width, then you may want to start with a 3 millimeter width in the background of the landscape. You may choose to utilize the open stitches in the background areas of the landscape for developing depth because they are less visible.

Keep in mind that the thread color also comes into play in creating depth. By matching the thread color with the fabric color, you will develop more depth.

You will blossom into your own sense of style with the stitches you use in your landscape. There is no right or wrong choice—it's a matter of personal preference. Since we are all born as unique individuals, we have different style preferences in designing landscapes. Your style is also reflected in the décor of your home and in the choice of clothing you wear. Some of us like muted, soft colors, while others prefer brilliant colors. These are simply our comfort zones in life.

Stitch Variations

Mirror Imaging

Many sewing machines have "bells and whistles" that we forget to use. One such feature is mirror imaging. Mirror imaging flips the stitch from top to bottom or side to side. With mirror imaging, you can completely change the look of a stitch and what it does for the landscape. This is an example of getting out of the box and rethinking things.

Pictured here is a stitch that works wonderfully for creating grass. You can find it in the decorative stitch program menu on your machine. When this stitch is mirror imaged from top to bottom, it is also very effective for creating texture or crevices along the ridge of the mountain. You can also use this feature to

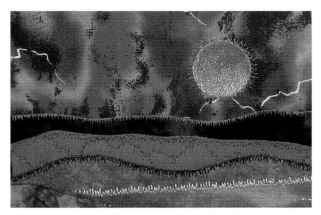

Mirror imaging changes the look of the stitches.

stitch rays around the sun/moon with the same stitch. This is just one example of what can be done with one basic stitch program and mirror imaging.

Maxi Stitches and Large Decorative Stitches

Many sewing machines offer additional large stitches called "maxi stitches" or "large decorative stitches." They are often referred to as "8-way" or "16-way" feed stitches. Some of these stitches are as wide as 60 millimeters. There are many of these stitch patterns that are great for landscape use—flowers, vines, leaves, animals, etc. They can be used in single patterns or stitched out in a sequence. Since these are very large designs, they come in handy for the embellishing details.

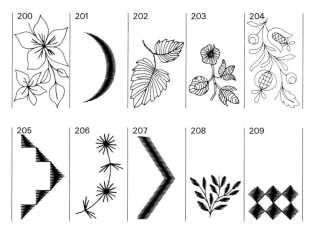

A sampling of maxi stitches from the Pfaff sewing machine manual. Reprinted by permission of Pfaff American Sales Corp.

Enlarged Stitches With a Software Program

Your machine may have a software program that allows you to change the stitch width and length of any of the stitch programs to a new pattern size.

The tan grass stitch enlarged to 20mm.

The tan grass stitch in this photo has been enlarged to 20mm. This is a quick and easy option and one you shouldn't overlook if your machine has that capability. Use your machine to its fullest potential and you'll enjoy it even more. The possibilities are endless as to what you can do to change the stitches with a software program and, oh, what fun!

Single Pattern Stitch

This decorative stitch creates a realistic looking fern plant.

Here are some examples of what can be done with the single pattern feature of your sewing machine. Many flower patterns can be combined with a leaf stitch or other stitch to form a patch of flowers. Or perhaps you have a stitch that looks like a fern when it is used as a single pattern, as shown in the photo. Check out your stitch menu to see what other possibilities you have. Review Chapter 8 on embellishment details for other ideas of what can be done with these stitches.

Twin Needle Stitching

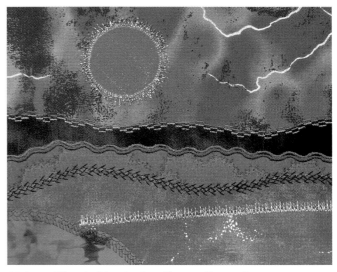

Twin needle stitching is visually very dynamic.

Using a twin needle provides another option for creating a different stitching style. This technique brings out a completely different perspective with any stitch. I used a 2.5 twin needle with these stitches and the results are so much fun!

Memory Programming a New Pattern Sequence

Another fun thing to do with stitches is to make up your own variations by combining stitch patterns in a new sequence.

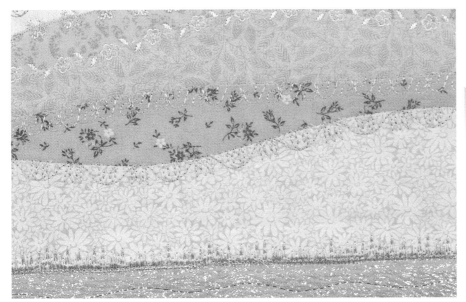

The new tulip stitch on the yellow daisy mountain was formed by programming one tulip stitch right side up, and the second tulip stitch upside down. When they are stitched out in a continuous sequence, this is the end result.

In the photo above, the yellow daisy mountain above the water shows a new stitch I programmed using the same stitch but mirror imaging one of the tulips. The pink mountain shows a new variation created by combining a leaf and flower stitch pattern. These are easy stitch changes to program into your machine. Again, just take the time to play with the stitches and you will come up with some wonderful ideas of your own.

Create a Stitch Notebook

Take the time to play with the stitches on your machine. See how they look stitched at different widths and lengths. You may want to try mirror imaging if you have that feature on your machine. And don't forget twin needle stitching. Sometimes we think we know our sewing machines well until we take the time to just doodle with the stitches. I am always pleasantly surprised by the new discoveries I make when I just relax and play with the stitches.

One of the most worthwhile projects you can do is to create a notebook of stitches for future reference. Although this takes some time to do now, it will reduce your sewing time later. The notebook is a handy reference to help you

You've heard of doodling on paper. Try doodling with your machine stitches on fabric! This is my experimental stitch notebook.

quickly decide which stitch to use. It is a very useful tool, not only in designing landscapes, but for other projects as well.

I created my notebook by stitching over the raw edges of strips of fabric. This doesn't have to be pretty—it is just an experiment to learn what your machine can do and how stitches look at different widths and lengths. It's important to stitch over the raw edges of a fabric strip rather than to just stitch on a piece of fabric because stitching the raw edges helps you see the contrast and transition from one fabric to another as well as the stitch placement along the raw edge. By doing this, you can preview what will happen when you construct a landscape with that stitch. Use a fabric-marking pen to note on your sample the stitch program number and the stitch width and length. This will save you a lot of sewing time later, since you won't have to spend time running many test samples of different stitches. You can quickly look at your notebook and determine what stitch you want to use.

Stitch Placement

As a rule, stitches should be positioned directly over the fabric join, but of course there are exceptions. Many stitches form a center line that runs between the stitch patterns when

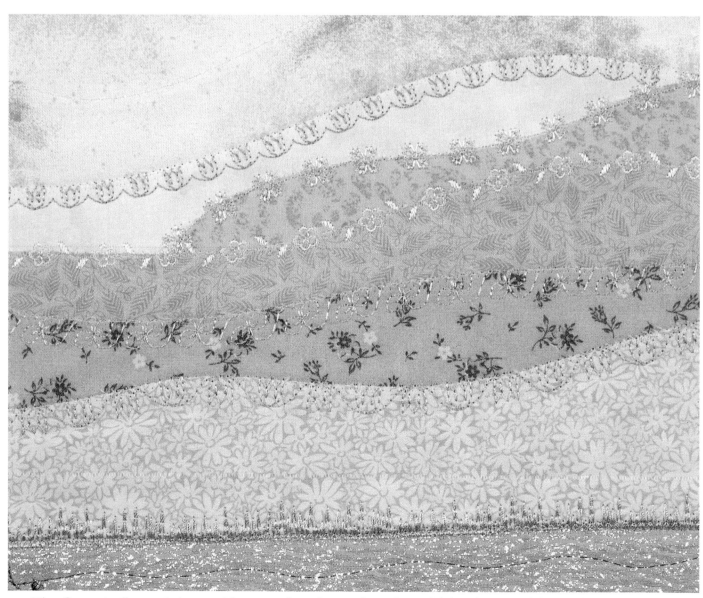

These decorative flower stitches are either centered on the raw edge or dropped below the curve of the raw edge.

you sew them. Flower, heart, and star stitches are good examples of the running stitch lines between the spaces of the pattern. This type of stitch looks best when the center line runs right along the raw edge and the flowers (or other patterns) fall in the middle of the two landscape pieces you are joining together.

In the photo on page 54, the pink flowers on the second green mountain are positioned along the raw edge. When the center line of the stitch pattern falls directly along the raw edge, the line becomes less obvious. This is kind of like simulating "stitching in the ditch," where you stitch in or next to a seam line to hide your stitching.

Some stitches look better placed just under the curve or the raw edge. For instance, look at the green tulip stitch on the top yellow mountain. This stitch shows up much prettier if it isn't falling partially into the sky area. This is another factor to consider when positioning your stitches. In this case, the raw edge of the mountain was stitched down first with monofilament thread and a zigzag stitch.

Stitch to Suit the End Use

Before you begin sewing your landscape, you should know how it will be used. This helps determine what type of stitches are appropriate. If a landscape is going to be sewn on the back of a garment, the stitches must be sturdy enough to withstand the abrasion of wearing it. Sliding in and out of the car, throwing your purse over your shoulder, or even putting on and taking off your coat causes a lot of additional wear and tear. For garment use, I like to use a stitch that is more closed and encases the raw edges better. The same is true if a landscape is to be used on a pillow front, tote bag, or on a purse. These items get tossed around a lot and are subject to more abuse.

If the landscape is going to be used as artwork for a wall hanging, it isn't as critical that you use a sturdy stitch. The decorative satin stitches are a good choice for sewing items that will be subjected to more abuse because they encase the raw edges much better.

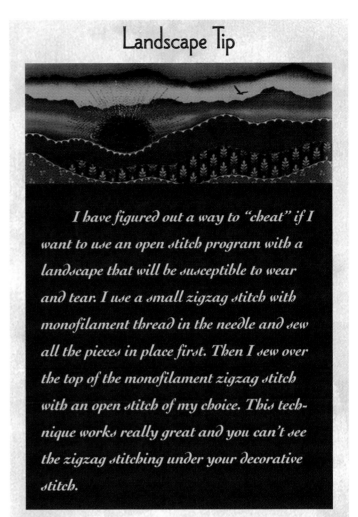

Landscape Tip

I have figured out a way to "cheat" if I want to use an open stitch program with a landscape that will be susceptible to wear and tear. I use a small zigzag stitch with monofilament thread in the needle and sew all the pieces in place first. Then I sew over the top of the monofilament zigzag stitch with an open stitch of my choice. This technique works really great and you can't see the zigzag stitching under your decorative stitch.

If you don't know what you are going to do with a landscape when you begin, it is always a safe bet to stitch it first with the monofilament zigzag technique given in the Landscape Tip at right. Then you will have more flexibility as to its end use.

Thread Choices

i'm very excited about all the varieties of threads we have at our fingertips today. My threads, just like my fabric stash, are my treasures! I really enjoy looking at thread color cards and seeing all the choices available. The colors are fascinating and it feels kind of like going into a candy store and drooling over the selection of goodies in front of me. I just haven't figured out how I can get a sugar fix from looking at those enticing thread color cards yet.

These days there are just about as many varieties of threads as there are fabrics. Knowing how to use all of these wonderful threads is as important as learning how to use the decorative stitches. Threads and decorative stitches really go hand in hand. Of course, needle choices, thread tension, and the proper foot on your machine also come into play for a successful project. There are many good books available that address these issues in much more depth than this book. Refer to page 127 for a recommended reading list.

Landscapes provide a wonderful opportunity to incorporate all types of different threads for embellishment. Think of threads as the "paint" that enables you to create special effects, just like an artist does with the paint palette. Always keep an open mind about the threads you see and how to use them. Step out of the box and be creative. In addition to the rayon threads commonly used for decorative stitches, there are many other options. If the thread is too large to go through the needle, try some reverse bobbin work using decorative cords, pearl crown rayon, ribbon floss, yarns with slubs, Monet, silk ribbon, and metallics, to name a few. Does this get your thought processes going?

How you use threads is a matter of personal preference. Any type of thread, just like fabric, should be viewed as a candidate for landscape construction. Various assortments of threads can be used to help create definition, contrast, texture, highlighting, and reflection.

There is a "candy store of thread" choices available.

Threads basically fall into two categories. First are the ones that are fine enough to go through the eye of the needle and second are the heavier threads that must be wound on a bobbin and applied through reverse bobbin work or by couching them on.

Threads Through the Needle

Use the appropriate needle for the threads you are sewing with. It takes some time and practice to get to know the idiosyncrasies of the various threads. If the needle is too small for the thread, the thread will fray or even break. If a needle is too large for the thread, the stitches will be distorted and will leave noticeable needle holes. If you hear a punching or thumping sound as the machine is sewing, the needle may be dull or have a burr on it. In this case, change the needle immediately. It's a good idea to start a new project with a new needle. I keep a good supply of embroidery needles on hand because they are the ones I use the most. They work well for sewing decorative stitches, as well as stitching machine embroidery designs from software cards.

You will also want to have some metallic needles for metallic threads and some topstitch needles in case you want to put two threads through the eye of the needle. If you are having trouble with a thread that shreds, even with a new needle, try a 90/14 topstitch needle that has a larger eye.

Since most of the construction process utilizes decorative stitches, you will use a lot of rayon decorative threads. I primarily use 40-weight rayon threads. Stock a basic supply of assorted colors because you will use a lot of them. There is nothing more frustrating than being ready to start sewing and not having what you need at your fingertips. An investment in thread now will save cherished sewing time later.

In some cases, you may want to use regular construction thread rather than decorative rayon thread. Regular thread is a good choice for areas of the landscape where you prefer thread without shine.

I also use many metallic threads for special effects. If a thread feels bumpy or rough as you pull it between your fingers, you will need to use a metallic or topstitch needle. The metallics do a magnificent job of producing rays around a sun/moon or creating waves and highlights on the water. I suggest using a lightweight polyester or nylon thread in the bobbin when using metallic thread in the top needle. The lightweight bobbin thread helps prevent metallic thread from getting hung up, thereby reducing breakage problems.

Needle threads.

Flat polyester film threads.

Bobbin threads.

Flat polyester films, such as Madeira Jewel, Sulky Sliver, or Glitter, will produce a brilliant reflection in the water. They should be placed in a vertical position when feeding them through the machine. I often use two different colors of thread through the needle. To do this, set the machine up with a stitch length of 4.0 and a topstitch needle. The longer stitch length is important to produce more reflection from the thread. When the two threads are combined, they will twist back and forth as you sew. You will see a glimmer of both colors and the reflection is much greater.

I recommend using two threads through the needle when sewing water, whether you use the same or different colors. Two threads are much more reflective and dynamic than a single thread. See Chapter 8 on embellishments for more detail and photos.

Threads Through the Bobbin

There are many threads manufactured today specifically for use in the bobbin. Bobbin threads are available in several weights and fiber contents. When sewing with decorative stitches, the stitches cause a buildup of thread on the top and bottom of your fabric. Using special lightweight bobbin thread helps minimize the buildup of thread under the fabric.

I've found that different brands of sewing machines function better with certain weights of bobbin thread. Experiment with your machine to find out what bobbin thread weight and fiber works the best. The bobbin screw in your bobbin case can be adjusted to accommodate different weights of thread. (I always remember which way to turn the screw by the saying "righty tighty and lefty loosy.") A general rule for the bobbin thread is to use the same weight for the bobbin as is in the needle.

Threads for Reverse Bobbin Work

Use reverse bobbin work when threads are too large to go through the eye of the needle. For this technique, the thread is wound on a bobbin, placed in the bobbin case, then sewn with the right side of the fabric face down on the machine (toward the feed dogs). As you sew, you are looking at the wrong side of the fabric, so it's a work of faith because you can't see what's going on underneath. I'm like a little kid when I do this—I sew a few inches, then peek under the fabric to see what kind of magic is going on. Hopefully, it's something good! If you haven't tried this technique, I think you'll find it fascinating and certainly worth the effort. Like everything else, it may take some practice.

Threads that work well with reverse bobbin work are metallic braids or cords, Pearl Crown rayon, embroidery floss, ribbon floss, and flat braids. There are many to choose from for this purpose.

The grass stitching was done with reverse bobbin work using a smooth twisted rayon thread.

The grass in the photo was created using reverse bobbin work and Pearl Crown rayon thread by YLI. It is an easy thread to practice with because it is a smooth twisted rayon that doesn't snag easily as it passes through the tension spring. It's just one of many thread choices that could be used for creating grass.

When doing reverse bobbin work, remember that the needle thread will show up as little dots on top of the bobbin work. Choose the needle thread according to the look you want to achieve with the bobbin work. The needle thread can contrast, blend, or be invisible (monofilament). Sometimes the needle threads appear to float on the surface of the right side of the fabric. Longer stitch lengths are usually easier to use and show up better. You may need to tighten the top tension to compensate for the loose bobbin tension necessary for reverse bobbin work. Of course, you should run a test before you start stitching with reverse bobbin work on your landscape.

It's a good idea to have an extra bobbin case filled with the heavier thread for reverse bobbin work. Your sewing machine tension must be adjusted to accommodate the extra thread weight and a second bobbin case enables you to keep your regular bobbin case set for normal sewing without changing the tension. Since the weight of the thread used for reverse bobbin work is so drastically different than regular sewing thread, the second bobbin case will allow you to play with the tension as needed.

Threads for Couching

Couching is a technique where the thread is laid on the surface of the fabric and stitched on with a zigzag or decorative stitch. Threads that won't go through the bobbin case can be applied by couching them on. These are threads that are too large or have slubs of thread that won't pass through the tension spring. The needle thread can be blending, contrasting, or invisible. You will need to use a special couching foot that has a sizable groove under the foot for the heavy threads to pass through easily.

Threads that are too large for the needle and bobbin can be couched on.

If you are going to use heavier threads, either through the bobbin case or by couching them on, take into consideration where you are going to place them on the landscape. Due to their visible size and texture, they should be incorporated closer to the foreground area. They are very helpful for developing close-up detail, which in turn also helps create depth.

Choosing Threads

After I have cut out all the landscape pieces, I am ready to start making decisions about which threads I want to use. I like to arrange all the fabric pieces on my cutting table, from the top to the bottom, according to the design layout. At this point, I get a first glance at the landscape and a feeling for what I want to develop with the threads through the stitches. How do the fabrics in the landscape read when you view them? Is there a mood or a feeling that the landscape projects? I like to make my decisions about the threads and stitches by what I perceive at this stage. The thread choices are important because they help to convey or carry out my first impression.

When I first started constructing landscapes with decorative threads, I chose threads by matching the fabrics with the thread colors. This seems to be a natural inclination—one I've observed often in my students. It's what we've been taught to do—match the fabric to the thread. But it's not necessarily the best way to go when stitching landscapes, as you will see.

Low Contrast Thread

Using low contrast thread simply means that you stitch the fabrics with the same color thread as the fabric—the black mountain is stitched with the black thread and the purple mountain is stitched with purple thread.

When the landscape is constructed with matching thread, there is very little contrast between the thread and the land shapes. The eye will move easily across the landscape as you view it. There is very little or no contrast using this approach for thread choices. Use low contrasting thread when you want the landscape to have a soft and subtle appearance. Low contrast threads are also very useful for developing depth in the background where you may want to minimize the mountains in the distance.

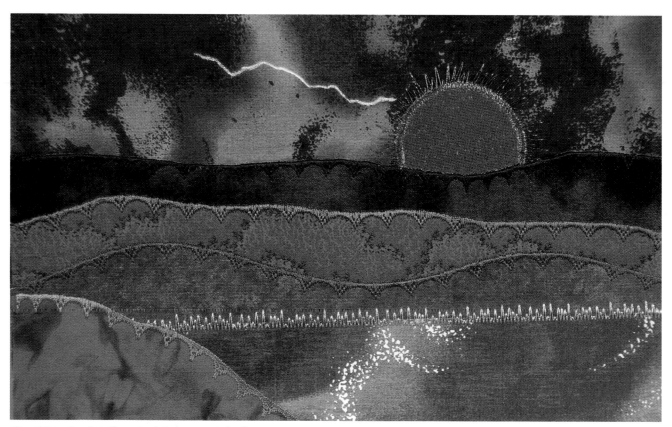

Matching the thread to the fabric creates little or no contrast.

High Contrast Thread

The second approach is to use threads that show up against the fabrics as a contrast—teal thread on a black mountain and purple thread on a teal mountain. By using this technique, you create a contrast between the fabric and the thread. The land shapes become more defined and the eye will stop and take notice.

The photo shows how the mountains stand out more when they are stitched with contrasting thread. I enjoy mixing up threads and using them to create a contrast rather than a blend. Use high contrast threads when you want to make a strong visual impact or draw attention to a specific detail.

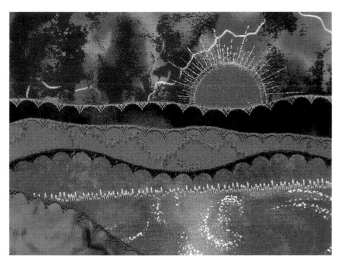

High contrast thread gives the features more definition.

No Contrast Thread

Occasionally when I design a landscape, I really like the first impression I see when the fabrics are placed in position without any stitching on them. Perhaps the effect is very soft and it seems like using decorative stitches may take away from the beauty rather than add to it. In that case, I use a zigzag stitch with monofilament thread in the needle.

After having experimented with many landscape designs, I prefer to match the fabrics to the threads, but also choose a couple threads that are slightly different in value (lighter or darker). I place all the threads on top of the landscape before I begin to sew. Then I mix them up and sew with a different color thread on each fabric, rather than a matching thread. That's my preference, but you may like the look of low or no contrast better. Remember, there's no right or wrong—if you like it, you did it right.

Good lighting is important when choosing threads and deciding how you will use them. I prefer to make thread decisions during the daylight hours when there is a lot of natural light coming into my sewing room. Otherwise, make sure you have good lighting from other sources—it can make such a difference in the design process.

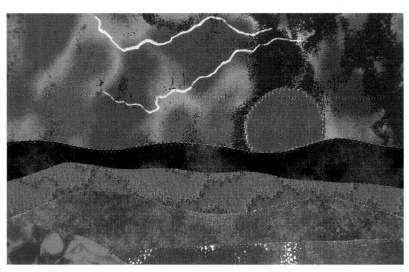

If you like the look of the fabrics against each other without stitching, use invisible (no contrast) thread.

Embellishing Techniques

𝓝ow for the fun—the embellishing details! For those of us who really enjoy embellishing, sometimes it becomes the "embellishing disease." Knowing when to stop is the key. I can always think of another detail that might be interesting to add, but at some point all the extras will begin to take away from the beauty of the original piece. I believe this is called "the law of diminishing returns."

Many of these embellishing methods help create close-up detail. By developing the detail on the foreground, the background will become more distant and that's what you want to achieve with embellishing techniques.

Machine Embroidery

Using the sewing machine embroidery design capabilities is so fun and exciting these days. This market has exploded and there is a design for almost anything you can think of. Many of the embroidery designs featured on the landscapes in this book are from my embroidery card, *Linda Crone Signature Landscape Elements* from Cactus Punch. These designs were developed specifically for land-

This sample shows 12 of the 25 designs on my Cactus Punch embroidery card.

scapes, although I have used many on garments as well. They are very helpful if you want to build some scenery with a house, church, or barn, etc.

Husqvarna also has a software program available called "ReSize Plus System 5." It can be used with all designs and sewing embroidery machine models. This exciting program will help you to get more mileage from your embroidery designs because you can resize them to fit your needs. ReSize Plus will increase or decrease the size of your embroidery design—keeping the stitch density constant while changing the stitch count to accommodate the new size.

The landscape quilt shown on page 62 is a sample I made for the Cactus Punch show display. It has 12 designs incorporated, which is more than I would normally use on one landscape. I tried to use as many designs as I could from the 23 designs on the software package. The fabrics for this landscape are mostly blenders, or small scale prints. Since I knew I wanted to feature as many embroidery designs as possible, I felt it was important for the background fabrics to be as subtle as possible.

The three-dimensional flowers on this landscape mimic the flowers in one of the companion fabrics used to decorate the room where it will hang.

Featured in the lower right corner of another landscape is a collage of flowers and leaves from my design card. The centers of the flowers are accented with thread beads. Any machine embroidery design that is an all-thread design can be stitched on a piece of organza and then trimmed close to the edges of the design. To do this, put the organza in the middle of two layers of water-soluble stabilizer. Stitch the design, remove the stabilizer, and trim away the organza.

Landscape Tip

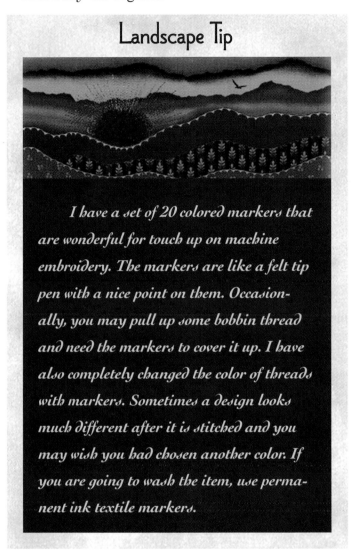

I have a set of 20 colored markers that are wonderful for touch up on machine embroidery. The markers are like a felt tip pen with a nice point on them. Occasionally, you may pull up some bobbin thread and need the markers to cover it up. I have also completely changed the color of threads with markers. Sometimes a design looks much different after it is stitched and you may wish you had chosen another color. If you are going to wash the item, use permanent ink textile markers.

Printed Fabrics

Even if you don't have an embroidery machine, you can still add wonderful embellishments to your landscape. Any design you can find on a printed fabric can be utilized in your landscape. I keep a collection of fabrics of flowers, rocks, grass, trees, etc., just for that purpose. In several of the landscapes in this book, you will see printed fabrics worked into the scene. It is important to keep the size of the fabric design in proportion to the scale of the landscape.

These tiny florals are a combination of the same print in two different color ways.

Before cutting out a fabric design, fuse HeatnBond Lite, a paper-backed fusible web, to the back of the fabric. Leave the paper on the back of the design while you trim around the edges. This technique is especially helpful with designs that are more complicated like the plants with the tiny blades of grass in the photo at left. By stabilizing the fabric with the fusible web, the cut edges will look much neater. Then remove the paper and fuse the design in place with your iron. Attach the design to the landscape with simple zigzag stitching around the edges of the fabric shape with monofilament thread in the needle. In some cases, it is easier to secure the design using free-motion embroidery (see Chapter 4, page 30). The photos show flowers, rocks, and blades of grass that have been added to a landscape by using printed fabric.

These rocks were trimmed around the shape of the rocks, then zigzagged in place with invisible monofilament thread.

Thread Painting

Thread painting is exactly what it sounds like—painting on fabric using threads as your paintbrush. It can be done as a free-motion stitch (see Chapter 4, page 30) or in the regular sewing mode with a straight stitch. With this technique, you can add a little bit of thread just for the highlights or you can thread paint the whole design.

These three grass plants added a touch of nature for the storks to wade through.

The lion in the foreground has a striking three-dimensional look due to heavy thread painting.

The highlighting on the lions, crevices in the hills, and the grass were created by free-motion thread painting

The lion in the photo above was cut from fabric and thread painted completely. The beard around the lion's face was stitched with several layers of straight stitches using YLI Monet thread. Some of the stitches were clipped, then the threads were brushed out with a wire brush to make the beard fuzzy. The lion is quite a handsome fellow!

The photos on pages 65 and 66 show some of the other animal fabric designs that were highlighted with thread. The bird was traced from a picture, then the outline was transferred to fabric and free-motion stitched on the landscape.

Batting under the rocks accentuates the free-motion highlighting of the rocks, tiger, and grass.

Sometimes it's difficult to find just the "right" bird from stock embroidery designs. This bird was traced and created through thread painting to get the desired effect.

Rhinestones or Beads

Occasionally I like to add some tiny rhinestones to the center of flowers. It's the perfect place for just a little highlight.

The stones in the photo below are iron-on crystals. I like to use a few of them for added sparkle because they bring life to the landscape. It's just a little something that catches you by surprise when you notice them. Tiny glass beads also make great accents in the middle of flowers.

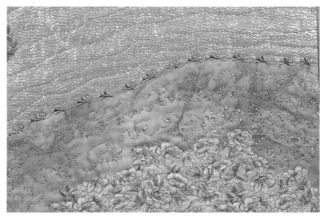

Reverse bobbin work creates wonderful added texture in this foreground.

Reverse Bobbin Work

The foreground of the landscape is a good place to add some pizzazz with reverse bobbin work. Because these are heavy threads that stand out, they need to be in the foreground.

The threads in the photo at right remind me of frosting drizzled on a cake. I used Madeira Décor thread and pulled it up through the wide opening in the bobbin case. I didn't pull the thread through the tension spring in the bobbin case as I normally would. Instead I used free-motion stitching and slowly moved the fabric around. Reverse bobbin work is done with the right side of the fabric facing down on the machine so you sew looking at the wrong side of the fabric. I call this technique a work of faith. It's always a surprise when you turn the fabric right side up to see how it looks.

Flower centers are one of my favorite spots to highlight with rhinestones.

Fabric Layering

When stitching the landscape in the photo below, I put a layer of white sheer organza fabric over the pink batik fabric. If you have a fabric that isn't quite the color you want, try experimenting with organza and netting. These fabrics are very sheer and can help lighten or darken a fabric. In this case, the pink fabric was brighter than I wanted and the white organza softened the appearance.

The water fabric in the bottom photo is a combination of two different fabrics—an iridescent crinkled organza on top of green fabric. In this case, the organza was shaded to a different color. By putting the green fabric underneath, it changed the color of the organza from a turquoise to a soft green. Actually, I used the same green fabric that was in the top green mountain in the photo below. I reversed the fabric and used the wrong side so the print wouldn't show through the organza.

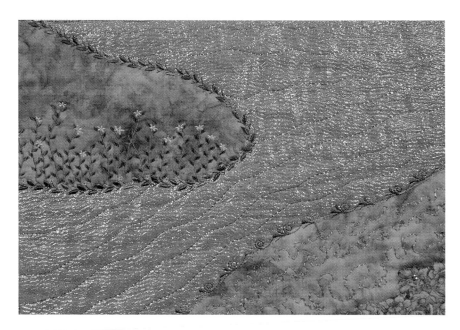

The crinkled organza fabric used for the water displays a rippled water effect.

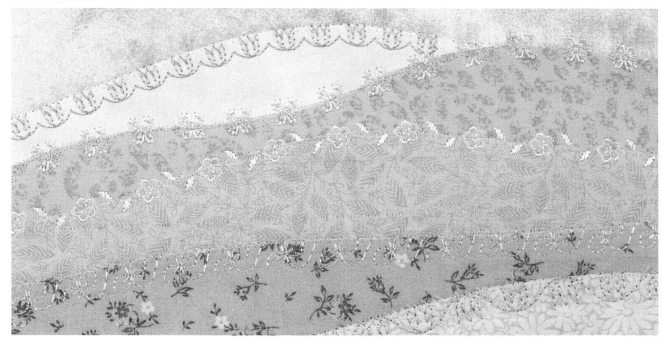

The green mountain fabric has a mottled print on it, but the back of the fabric was just perfect for the shading technique.

Grass Using Fabric or Threads

I like to add grass to the foreground because it adds a beautiful three-dimensional look. Here are two different ways to make grass.

Here I used a strip of fabric to create the grass by fringing the raw edges. In fact, I added two layers of grass. When fringing, a fabric with a coarse grain makes a thicker fringe. Fabrics with a high thread count per square inch don't fringe well because the threads are too fine and they tend to clump together. In this landscape, the grass fabric is made with a coarse weave home dec fabric.

Making your own fringe for grass is very quick and easy to do.

1 Measure the landscape to see how long a grass strip you need to cover the foreground.

2 Cut a strip of fabric 1-1/2″ wide, on the straight of grain, the length you need. With wrong sides together, fold the strip in half lengthwise.

3 Begin fringing by pulling away the threads from the edges of both long sides. Keep pulling threads until you are 1/4″ from the folded edge.

4 Pin the foreground on the landscape. Tuck the 1/4″ folded edge of the grass under the raw edge of the foreground piece. Pin the grass in place.

5 Stitch over the raw edge of the foreground, securing the grass in place. Choose a stitch that will encase the raw edge well. I used an overlock stitch.

Grass created with a fringe foot is fluffy and three-dimensional.

For this landscape, I created grass using three different colors of green rayon thread. I used a specialty sewing machine foot called a fringe foot and a zigzag stitch. The fringe foot has a center bar that forms loops as you zigzag over the top of it. Check with your sewing machine dealer to purchase one of these feet if you don't have one.

1 Zigzag stitch the foreground fabric in place along the raw edge.

2 Set up your machine for a zigzag stitch with a very short stitch length (0.5) and a width just wide enough to jump over the bar on both sides (2.0-3.0).

3 Sew the first row of loops on top of the edge of the foreground. Lightly press the loops up to get them out of the way for the second row.

4 Change thread colors if you wish and stitch the second row of loops very close to the first row. Again, lightly press them up.

5 Change thread and stitch the third row of loops close to the second row.

6 On the wrong side of the landscape, use fabric glue or fuse a narrow strip of fusible interfacing on the three rows of stitching to help secure the loops in place.

7 On the right side, hold a steam iron about 3″ above the fabric and release a few bursts of steam to perk up the threads. Don't iron or press the loops.

8 Clip some of the loops to create the look of grass. I clipped about 2/3 of the loops. The unclipped loops help fluff up the rest.

Landscape Tip

If you want the grass to be thicker, use two threads through the needle as you sew over the fringe foot.

Stenciling & Stamping

As you thumb through this book, you'll notice several birds in the landscapes. These birds were stenciled using black Shiva Oil Sticks and a brass stencil. There are lots of stenciling and stamping images available if you want to include them in your landscapes.

The rubber stamps shown in the photo are excellent choices to utilize in landscapes. The images of leaves and trees could easily be stamped in the foreground of the landscape. You can use any paint recommended for use on fabrics for the landscapes.

I frequently use bird stencils for the small birds in the sky. There's a wide selection of stencils available that will work with your landscape scenery.

Stenciled ducks nestled in the grass.

These rubber stamps present landscaping opportunities. These are from Rubber Stampede, Posh Impressions, and Hero Arts.

The goose was done with stencils and Shiva Oil Sticks.

There are lots of stencils that can be used for landscapes as well. The stencil in the upper left is from The Stencil Collection. All the others are from American Traditional Stencils.

The birds in the sky were added with stencils.

Waves in the Water

Flat film threads add great reflective quality to waves in the water.

I usually add a layer of thin cotton batting under the water fabric before stitching it on the landscape. The batting gives dimension to the water and makes the threads more visible. I like to use flat film threads like Madeira Jewel, Sulky Sliver, or Glitter threads for the waves in the water. I prefer using two different colors of thread in the needle for this effect. To do this, I use a topstitching or metallic needle, and a straight stitch with a stitch length of 4.0 to stitch the waves. Stitch the entire body of water before you add the next pieces in the landscape. As you sew, gently swing the fabric back and forth to create the wavy lines.

Painted Sky Fabric

I have had very little experience with painting and dying fabrics and I don't claim to be an expert, but sometimes painting or dying is the only way to get the look I want, especially for skies.

One day, out of frustration because I couldn't find the right sky fabric in my stash, I decided to experiment. The only paint in my house was a collection of Delta Ceramcoat acrylic paints I used to paint on wood years ago. I read the side of the bottle and it said I could use the paint on fabric, so I made color washes with about a nickel's worth of paint and a scant 1/8 cup water each. I started with a dry piece of white muslin and painted some streaks of three different color washes side-by-side. I completely soaked the fabric with the color washes. As the fabric dried, it started to form lacy edges in some areas. I was surprised at the results. Now I know if I am really in a pinch for a sky fabric, I can simply use three paints that pick up the colors in the landscape and create my own.

The fabric before I started painting.

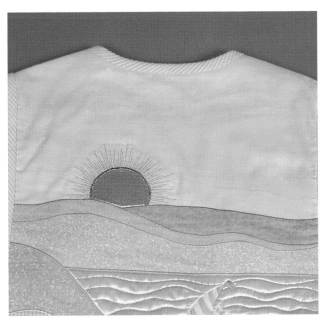

The pastels in this sky present a very peaceful, calming mood.

For the sky pictured below, I started with tan fabric that was mottled looking to begin with. I used three paints—yellow/gold, maroon, and forest green, all colors from the base fabrics in the bedroom where the landscape would hang. These paints seemed like an odd color combination at the time, but they turned out great. The sky appears to be reflect-ing the colors from the mountains. The clouds floating in the sky are pieces of tulle netting.

The sky fabric on the vest back above was painted to coordinate with the base garment fabric—a pastel striped seersucker. I used a combination of three paints—very soft pink, blue, and mint green. You can see the results are lovely.

After adding washes of yellow/gold, maroon, and forest green

Sun/Moon Techniques

The bronze lamé fabric for this sun enhances the sky fabric.

I like to use tissue lamé fabric to make the sun and moon. Since it has a wonderful shine, this fabric is the perfect medium for reflections. However, you can use any type of fabric and it doesn't necessarily need to have a brilliant shine. Tissue lamé is very delicate to work with and should be backed with a lightweight fusible interfacing. Always use a cool iron with lamé.

1 Cut a square piece of fabric large enough for the sun/moon.

2 Back the fabric with a lightweight fusible interfacing. I use lightweight fusible tricot.

3 Iron a piece of Wonder Under Light Fusible Web over the tricot. Leave the paper on the back and cut out the circle for the sun/moon (use a circle template if you have one). I use a 3″ circle for 17″ x 23″ landscapes, and a 1-3/4″ circle for 8″ x 10″ landscapes. The sun/moon should be large enough to make a statement without overpowering the scene. Try several paper template circle sizes in the sky to choose a size. This is a judgment call. Keep in mind that the sun/moon will appear larger once you sew the rays around it.

4 Decide where to place the sun/moon. You may wish to tuck it behind a mountain or place it in full view in the sky. If you want to position the sun behind the mountain, tuck it in

first, then sew across the mountain. If you've already sewn on the mountains, you could cut the sun/moon circle to fit the shape of the mountain, but this is difficult to do and achieve great results! Remove the paper backing. Place a pressing cloth over the sun/moon, and fuse the circle in place with a cool iron.

5 To stitch rays, start just inside the raw edge and stitch back and forth all the way around. You can use the forward and reverse method (sew forward, push the reverse button) or you can do it with free-motion stitching (drop the feed dogs and move the fabric back and forth). If you are using metallic or Sliver thread, use a long stitch length (4.0) to get more reflection from the thread. Make sure there is a stabilizer under the sun/moon to support the stitches.

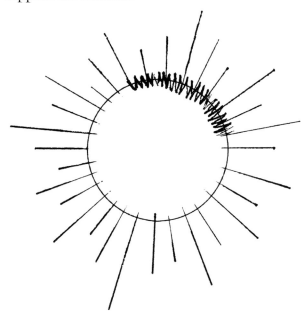

To stitch rays, start the stitching point just inside the circle. Zigzag over the stitch points and raw edges.

6 Zigzag satin stitch around the edge of the sun/moon as shown in the diagram. The stitch width should be at 3.0-4.0 and the length at about 0.5-1.0. This stitch covers the stitch points and raw edges of the sun/moon and creates a nice clean finish.

Clouds Floating Over the Sun/Moon

I like to float clouds over the sun/moon to create a realistic sky. I use a circle template to determine the size of the sun/moon and where to position it or I make a template from a piece of cardboard.

1 Follow the directions on page 74 to make the sun/moon.

2 Using the same size circle as the sun/moon, move a circle template around on the sky fabric until you see a pleasing configuration of clouds. What you see inside the template circle is the part of the sky (clouds) that will overlap the sun/moon. Use a disappearing ink pen or chalk to mark the circle on the sky fabric. Outline the clouds where they will be trimmed away from the fabric.

Draw a circle on the sky fabric with a disappearing ink pen.

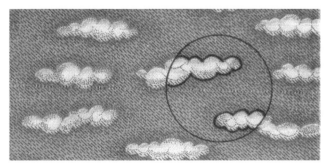

Outline the clouds where they will be cut away from the fabric.

3 On the wrong side of the sky fabric, iron a small piece of Wonder Under Lite Fusible Web on the cloud section that will be trimmed. Leave the paper backing on to make the trimming easier.

4 Trim the clouds on the inside of the circle up to the edge of the circle line. The photo shows the clouds outlined in black where you would trim. Peel the paper backing off the clouds and sun/moon.

Cut the portions of the clouds that will cover the sun/moon away from the sky fabric so they can be lifted up and placed on the top surface of the sun/moon.

5 Lift up the flaps of the clouds and slide the sun/moon under them. Use a cool iron with a press cloth to fuse the clouds in place. Turn the sky fabric to the wrong side and press again from the back.

Slide the sun/moon under the portions of the clouds that have been cut away.

6 With monofilament thread, zigzag over the raw edges of the cloud sections fused over the sun/moon.

7 Refer to the directions on page 74 and stitch rays around the sun/moon, skipping the sections around the edge where the cloud flaps overlap the sun/moon.

Mottled Land

The two closest mountains on the right have been highlighted with fabric patches to imitate mottled land.

When you look at mountains or scenery in the distance, the land often has a shadowed or mottled look to it. I like to combine a couple of different fabrics with a base fabric and layer small irregularly shaped patches over the base to duplicate this mottled effect. The mountains in the landscape above were constructed with this technique.

Cut the fabrics into several small irregularly shaped patches and arrange the patches in a pleasing design. Use temporary fusible spray to secure them in place. Zigzag or free-motion stitch around the patches to catch the edges. Use monofilament or contrasting thread, whichever you prefer. I added some extra stitching detail over the patches.

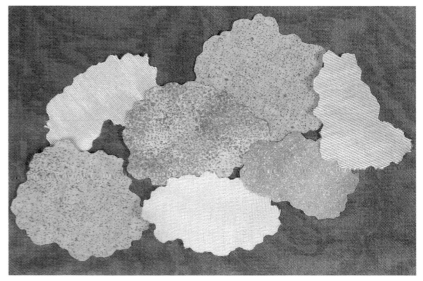

Cut the patches from fabrics that work well with each other and the base fabric.

Dimension With Batting

There are two places in landscapes where I use batting. I put one thin layer under the water section to give the waves more dimension and to give the threads more impact. I have constructed water with and without batting, and found that I prefer batting unless the landscape is very small. I also include one or two layers of batting under the foreground to help advance it forward visually. If you decide to do some contour stitching or quilting around flowers, the batting gives the foreground a nice three-dimensional look.

You may be tempted to put batting under the clouds in the sky. I don't do this because the extra dimension visually advances the clouds forward and the objective is to make them look more distant.

Fence With Felt

This easy-to-make fence is very effective when it is placed in the foreground of a landscape. This fence was created with a piece of felt fabric.

Fuse the back of the felt with a lightweight piece of fusible web. Cut out some jagged fence posts and fuse them to the landscape on the foreground. Cut some narrow strips of felt for the horizontal cross boards of the fence. These strips should be approximately half the width of the fence posts and the length you need to fit between the fence posts. Fuse the horizontal cross boards in place, butting the edges up next to the fence posts. Using a contrasting thread color, stitch on the fence posts and cross boards with a free-motion straight stitch.

This fence was laid out to make one of the horses appear to be escaping out the gate.

Beads Made of Thread

Thread beads look like real glass beads.

This is a great technique if you don't happen to have beads handy for embellishment. The accents on this tree are French knots, just like the ones made with embroidery floss. French knots can also be made with a heavy cord or braid of thread such as Madeira Glamour, Kreinik, or YLI Candelight. Thread beads also work well for the eyes of an animal or bird and I have used them in the center of a flower.

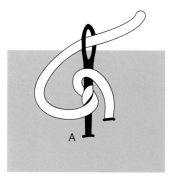

French knot.

Four Sample Landscape Projects

Chapter 9

Before You Start

It is very important to clear away everything around your sewing machine before you start sewing. The stitches on your landscape can easily become distorted if the landscape gets hung up on something near the sewing machine as it passes through the feed dogs (I speak from experience!). Let the feed dogs pull the fabric through the sewing machine and use your hands to gently guide the fabric. It's easy to apply too much pressure with your hands by trying to maneuver the fabric, thereby distorting the stitches. Relax and let your machine do the work.

You will need a piece of tracing paper or waxed paper, a pencil, scissors or rotary cutter, muslin, stabilizer, temporary spray adhesive (optional), fusible web, cotton lightweight batting (optional), and some pins. I like to use temporary spray adhesive rather than pins because it does a much better job of keeping the pieces from slipping. Of course, you will also need the fabrics for the landscape and decorative threads to go with your fabrics.

The instructions that follow arc for specific landscapes but the same construction techniques apply, no matter what landscape you're making. The differences lie in the pattern and the embellishments. The construction process is the same whether you are making a landscape for a picture, garment, or a quilt. Build the landscape on a piece of muslin fabric and a same-size piece of stabilizer.

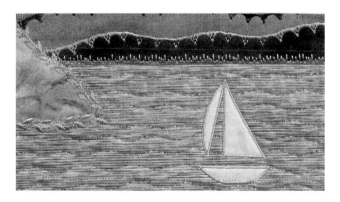

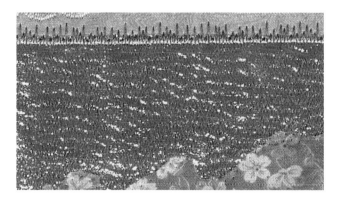

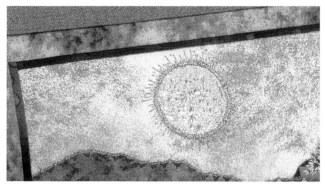

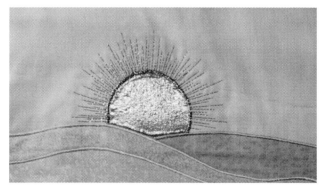

Step-by-Step Instructions for "Sail Away"

This sky fabric is an awesome piece of fabric to plan a landscape around.

The "Sail Away" landscape is made from the patterns on pages 84-86. The finished size is 8″ x 10″, perfect for a standard 8″ x 10″ picture frame. Construct the landscape on a 10″ x 12″ piece of muslin backed with stabilizer. I added an extra inch around all four sides of the landscape, extending the pattern pieces and strips of fabric for the sky and water, so the pattern pieces will fit exactly on the 10″ x 12″ muslin base. The extra inch gives you an area on the side to practice your stitches when you begin sewing. It also provides additional space for trimming the landscape to 8″ x 10″ after the construction is completed.

MATERIALS

Scraps of 8 different fabrics (sky, water, sun, boat, island, 3 mountains)
10″ x 12″ piece of muslin
10″ x 12″ piece of stabilizer
(2) 3″ squares Wonder Under Lite Fusible Web
4-1/2″ x 12″ strip of thin cotton batting
Thread to match or contrast as desired
Metallic or Sliver thread for stitching waves
Pattern tracing paper or waxed paper
Pencil
Pins or temporary spray adhesive

Trace the Patterns

1 Use pattern tracing paper or waxed paper to trace the landscape line drawing on page 84. Trace all the lines including the outside borders, then add 2″ extra to the sky at the top, and 1″ to both sides and the bottom. You will use this drawing to correctly position the pattern pieces.

2 Use pattern tracing paper or waxed paper to trace the landscape pattern pieces (#1, #2, #3, #4, #5, #6) on pages 85- 86.

3 Cut out all the pattern pieces from the paper.

Cutting Instructions

1 Pin pieces #1, #2, #3, and #4 on fabrics of your choice and cut one of each.

2 Cut a 3″ square of fabric for the sun and another for the sailboat. Cut two 3″ squares of Wonder Under Lite Fusible Web and fuse them to the back of the fabrics for the sun and boat. (*Note:* if you are using lamé for the sun, fuse it first with tricot knit interfacing and a *cool iron*, then add the fusible web to the back of the interfacing.) Leave the paper on and cut out the sun (#5) and two boat pieces (#6). On the paper side of the sail for the boat, use a pencil or pen to draw the dotted cutting line on the sail shown on the pattern.

3 Cut one 5-1/4″ x 12″ strip for the sky.

4 Cut one 4-1/2″ x 12″ strip for the water.

Construct the Landscape

1 Pin the 10″ x 12″ piece of muslin on top of the 10″ x 12″ stabilizer (you can use temporary spray adhesive instead of pins if you prefer).

2 Lay the sky fabric strip on top of the muslin, lining up the raw edges along the top and sides. Pin or spray in place.

When positioning the strip of sky fabric, line up the raw edges along the top and sides of the muslin.

3 Use the line drawing as a guide to position Mountain #1. Match the raw edges on the left end of the pattern piece to the left side of the muslin. Choose a decorative stitch and stitch along the *top ridge only* of the mountain. I used the same decorative satin stitch for mountains #1, #2, and #3.

Match the left raw edge of Mountain #1 to the left edge of the muslin.

4 Position Mountain #2 over the top of the sky and Mountain #1. Once again, use the line drawing for positioning. Match the raw edges on the right end of the pattern piece to the right side of the muslin. Choose a decorative stitch and stitch along the *top raw edge only* of Mountain #2.

Match the right raw edge of Mountain #2 to the right side of the muslin.

5 Position Mountain #3 over the top of Mountain #2, using the line drawing as a guide. Choose a decorative stitch and stitch along the *top ridge only* of Mountain #3.

Use the line drawing to position Mountain #3.

6 Lay the strip of fabric for the water over Mountain #3. Use the line drawing as a guide to position the fabric piece along the water line. Measure down from the top of the sky to the water line on both ends. This measurement should be the same on both ends to make sure the water is level. Use a satin zigzag stitch or a decorative grass stitch and stitch a straight line along the top of the water fabric, catching the top 1/8″ edge of the water fabric.

7 Lift up the water fabric piece and lay a piece of thin cotton batting underneath. Cut the batting to the exact size of the water piece. Stitch waves with metallic or Sliver thread, swinging the fabric back and forth, side-to-side, as you sew to create waves. I use a long straight stitch set at about 4.0. Adding the batting and stitching waves is optional, but it really adds to the final effect.

Use batting under the water piece to add dimension to the water.

8 Position Island piece #4 over the water and mountain pieces, using the line drawing as a guide. Choose a decorative stitch and stitch along the raw edge of the top, side, and bottom of the island piece. I used a decorative leaf stitch around this hill.

The Island piece is the last of the land pieces to stitch on.

9 For the sailboat sail, clip on the dotted line almost all the way up to the tip of the sail, but not through the tip. Leave a few threads at the tip to keep it attached. Remove the paper backing, split the sail slightly apart, and fuse the sail and boat sections on the water. Stitch around the sailboat with a tiny zigzag stitch.

Place the boat on the water and fuse in place.

10 Position the sun and fuse it in place with a cool iron. Stitch the rays around the sun with metallic or Sliver thread using a long straight stitch set at about 3.0. Zigzag with a satin stitch all the way around the edge of the sun, hiding the starting and stopping points of the rays. If you like the look of the clouds partially covering the sun, refer to page 75 in Chapter 8 for instructions.

Adding the sun is the final touch.

11 Turn the landscape over and remove the stabilizer, holding the stitches as you gently tear it away. Be very careful so the stitches don't become distorted when you pull away the stabilizer.

12 When pressing, be very careful not to put too much pressure on the iron or you'll leave an iron imprint on the fabric. Use a cotton/wool setting on your iron. You may opt to lightly press the landscape as you add each piece, but it shouldn't need it if you have a firm stabilizer.

13 Your landscape is now ready to be squared up. Refer to page 102 for directions. If you want to put it in a purchased 8″ x 10″ picture frame, simply trim the landscape to that size and slip it into the frame.

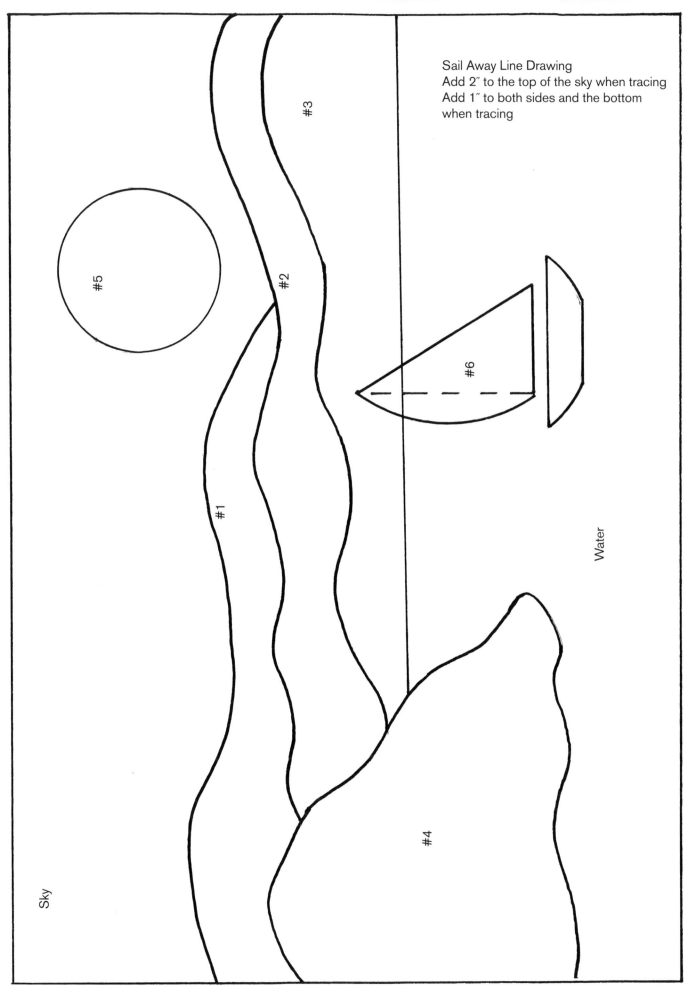

Sail Away Line Drawing
Add 2″ to the top of the sky when tracing
Add 1″ to both sides and the bottom
when tracing

#3

#5

#2

#6

#1

Water

#4

Sky

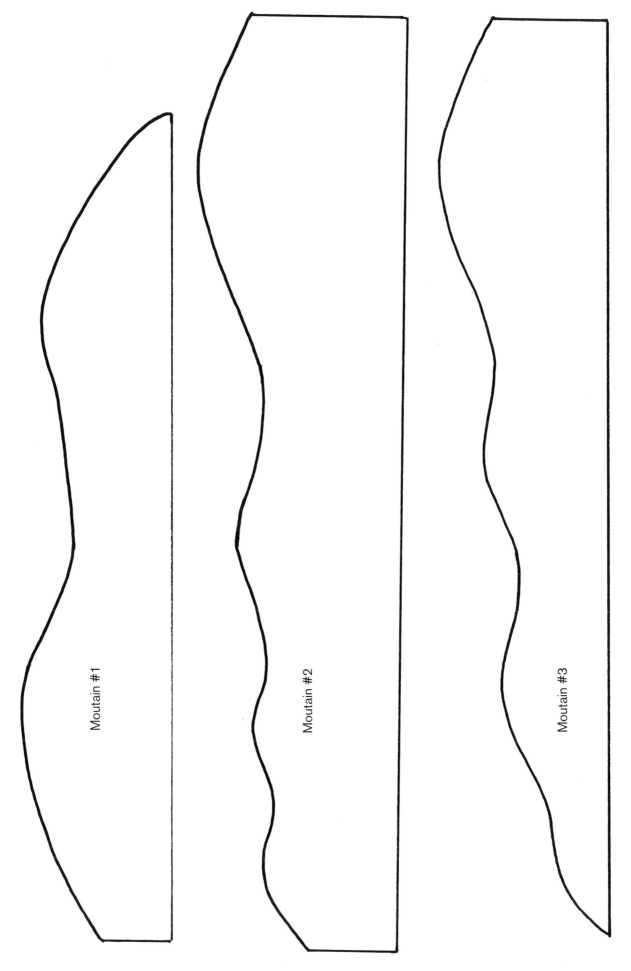

Moutain #1

Moutain #2

Moutain #3

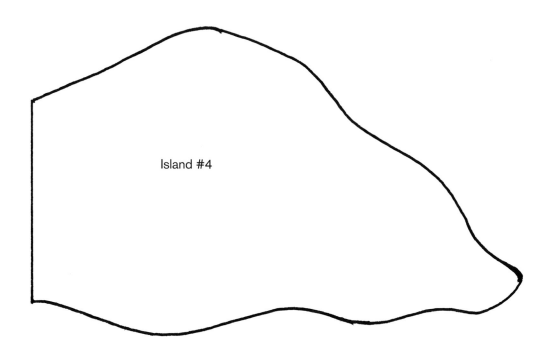

Island #4

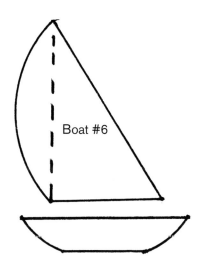

Boat #6

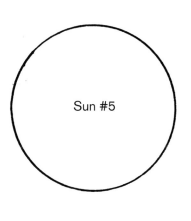

Sun #5

Step-by-Step Instructions for "Mini Seascape"

This little landscape makes a personal and meaningful greeting card for someone special. Make more than one at a time so you'll have them on hand for unexpected card-giving occasions. The water in this seascape is a combination of two fabrics: lamé on the bottom and crinkled organza on the top. Instead of cutting the foreground according to the cutting line, I trimmed around some of the flowers to make it look more interesting. The upper left corner of the card is embossed with a brass stencil and painted with watercolor paints.

This little pattern is very quick and easy. The greeting card is a special die-cut, tri-fold card called "Make It, Send It" by Linda Crone Creations, or you can make your own card with the instructions on page 89. The landscape pattern size is 6″ x 8″ and is designed to insert into the greeting card. However, you could trim the landscape to 5″ x 7″ and place it in a standard sized picture frame if you prefer.

Refer to the construction directions for "Sail Away" on page 81 for step-by-step photos of the construction process.

MATERIALS

Landscape

6″ x 8″ piece of muslin

6″ x 8″ piece of stabilizer

Scraps of 5 different fabrics
    (sky, 3 mountains, water)

Thread to match or contrast as
    desired

Pattern tracing paper or waxed paper

Pencil

Pins or temporary spray adhesive

Card

Die-cut "Make It, Send It" card

Or to make your own card:

8″ x 18″ piece of heavy paper (cardstock 65 to 80 lb.)

2 sheets 8-1/2″ x 11″ typing paper

Glue stick

Scissors, ruler, pencil, ballpoint pen

Stencil of choice

Water color or stencil paint

Stencil brush

Trace the Patterns

1 Use pattern tracing paper or waxed paper to trace the landscape line drawing on page 90. You will use this for positioning the pieces in the landscape.

2 Use pattern tracing paper or waxed paper to trace pattern pieces #1, #2, and #3 on page 91.

3 Cut out all the pattern pieces from the paper.

Cutting Instructions

1 Pin pattern pieces #1, #2, and #3 on fabrics of your choice and cut one of each.

2 Cut one 4″ x 6″ strip for the sky.

3 Cut one 2-1/2″ x 6″ strip for the water.

Construct the Landscape

1 Pin the muslin on top of the stabilizer or use temporary spray adhesive.

2 Place the sky fabric strip on top of the muslin, matching the raw edges at the top and sides. Spray with temporary spray adhesive or pin the fabric in place.

3 Position Mountain #1 on the sky fabric, matching the raw edges on the sides. Lay the line drawing tracing on top of the landscape to position the piece correctly. Choose a decorative stitch and stitch along the mountain *top edge only*. I used a satin decorative stitch for both Mountains #1 and #2.

4 Position Mountain #2 on top of Mountain #1, matching the raw edges on the sides. Use the line drawing for positioning. Choose a decorative stitch and stitch along the *top edge only* of Mountain #2.

5 Position the water strip over Mountain piece #2. Make sure it is straight by using the line drawing for guidance. Zigzag stitch or use a grass stitch to catch 1/8″ of the top edge only.

6 Place Mountain #3 over the water, matching the raw edges on the sides and bottom. Choose a decorative stitch to stitch it in place. I used a zigzag monofilament stitch because I didn't want it to show around the flowers. I chose to cut around the flowers rather than follow the cutting edge for the pattern piece.

7 Refer to page 102 for squaring up instructions and trim your landscape.

Make Your Own Card

1 On the wrong side of the 8″ x 18″ piece of cardstock, draw two fold lines very lightly with pencil. Draw the first fold line 6″ from the left edge, and the second 12″ from the left edge, dividing the 18″ length into three 6″ sections.

Draw 2 fold lines 6″ and 12″ from the edge

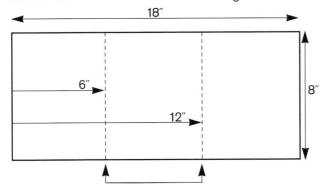

Score and fold toward the center.

2 Place a ruler along the fold lines and press a dry ballpoint pen (or similar tool that will create an indent without cutting the paper) along the line. Fold the card into thirds along the two scored lines, folding toward the center

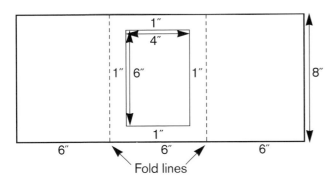

Fold lines

3 Open the card and on the center section, draw a light pencil line 1″ from all four edges. The measurement inside this "frame" is 4″ x 6″. Insert the tip of the scissors into the center of the 4″ x 6″ rectangle and cut it out.

4 Trim the "Mini Seascape" landscape to 5-3/4″ wide x 7-3/4″ high. Apply glue stick around the center opening on the back side of the card. Make sure to cover the inner edge of the opening with glue.

5 Wrong side up, center the landscape with the sky at the top in the opening of the card, and press around the four edges.

6 Place the card right side down on the table. Make sure the sky on the landscape is on top. Glue the left flap of the card with the glue stick, covering all the edges well and make an "x" in the middle. Fold the left flap of the card over the back of the landscape, pressing it firmly in place.

7 Fold the card in half and the landscape is now the front of the greeting card. Place the card under a heavy book for an hour to flatten.

8 If desired, stencil on the card front.

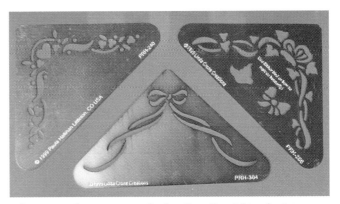

These stencils are custom designed to fit within the 1″ border of the greeting card. They really add a special soft touch to the perimeter of the card. Stencils by Linda Crone Creations.

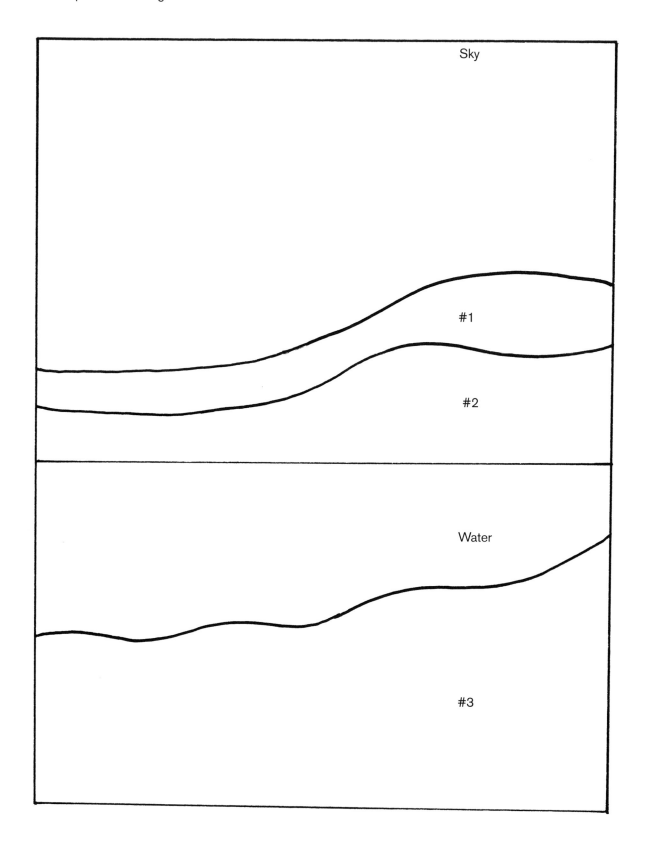

Sky

#1

#2

Water

#3

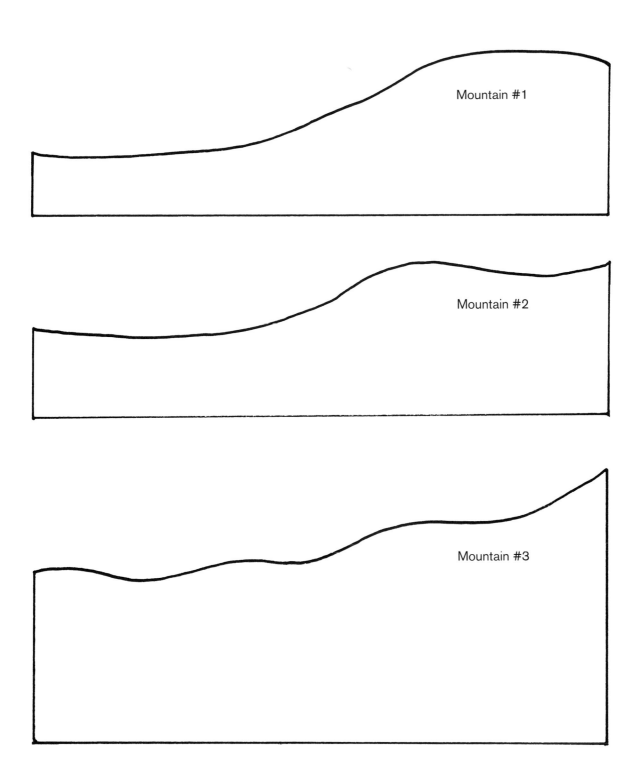

Mountain #1

Mountain #2

Mountain #3

Step-by-Step Instructions for "River Bend"

This landscape is different becuse it doesn't have a straight water line, so the water can be a river. The bag is made from Linda Crone Creations, pattern #106.

The actual size of the line drawing pattern is 7″ x 9″ and it is designed to fit in a 5″ x 7″ picture frame after trimming 1″ on all four sides. The photo shows the landscape sewn on a 10″ x 14″ tote bag. You may put this landscape on a ready-made 9″ x 11″ or larger tote bag.

Refer to the construction directions for "Sail Away" on page 81 for step-by-step photos of the construction process.

MATERIALS

7″ x 9″ piece of muslin
7″ x 9″ piece of stabilizer
Scraps of 9 different fabrics (sky, sun, river,
　　right river bank, 5 mountains)
Thread to match or contrast as desired

2″ square Wonder Under Lite Fusible Web
Pattern tracing paper or waxed paper
Pencil
Pins or temporary spray adhesive
Tote bag, 9″ x 11″ or larger

Trace the Patterns

1 Use pattern tracing paper or waxed paper to trace the landscape line drawing on page 96. You will use this for positioning the pattern pieces in the landscape.

2 Use pattern tracing paper or waxed paper to trace pattern pieces #1, #2, #3, #4, #5, #6, #7, and #8 on pages 97-98.

3 Cut out all the pattern pieces from the paper.

Cutting Instructions

1 Pin pattern pieces #1 through #7 on fabrics of your choice and cut one of each.

2 Cut a piece of batting from piece #6 (optional).

3 Cut a 2″ square of fabric for the sun and fuse it to the 2″ square of Wonder Under Lite Fusible Web. Pin pattern piece #8 on the fabric and cut out the sun.

4 Cut one 4″ x 9″ strip for the sky.

Construct the Landscape

1 Pin the muslin on top of the stabilizer or use temporary spray adhesive.

2 Place the sky fabric strip on the top of the muslin, matching the raw edges at the top and sides. Spray with temporary spray adhesive or pin the fabric in place.

3 Position Mountain #1 on the sky fabric, matching the raw edges on the left. Lay the line drawing on top of the landscape to position the piece correctly. Choose a decorative stitch and stitch along the curved line of the mountain *top edge only*. I used the same decorative satin zigzag stitch on Mountains #1, #2, #3, and #4.

4 Position Mountain #2 on the sky fabric, matching the raw edge on the right to the muslin edge. Use the line drawing for positioning. Choose a decorative stitch and stitch along the *top edge only*, following the curved line.

5 Position Mountain #3 over Mountain #2, matching the raw edges on the right. Choose a decorative stitch to stitch along the curved *top edge only*.

6 Position Mountain #4 in the middle, over Mountains #1, #2, and #3. Use the line drawing to position this piece. Choose a decorative stitch and stitch along the curved *top edge only*.

7 Position Mountain #5 over Mountains #1 and #4, matching the raw edges on the left. Choose a decorative stitch and stitch along the curved *top edge only*. I used a feather stitch.

8 Position River #6 over the top of Mountains #3, #4, and #5, matching the raw edges on the sides and bottom to the raw edges of the muslin base. Use a satin zigzag stitch to stitch along the curved top edge of the water. (*Note:* If you chose to use batting under the river, slide the batting under the river piece before you start stitching.)

9 Position Right River Bank #7 in the lower right corner, matching the raw edges at the bottom and right. Choose a decorative stitch and stitch along the curved top edge. You may want to use a satin zigzag stitch here also.

10 Remove the paper on the back of the sun. Position the sun and fuse it in place with the iron set at a cotton/wool setting. Stitch the rays around the sun with metallic or Sliver thread using a straight stitch set at 3.0 stitch length. Zigzag with a satin stitch all the way around the edge of the sun, hiding the starting and stopping points of the rays. If you like the look of the clouds partially covering the sun, refer to page 75 in Chapter 8 for instructions.

Add Embellishments

Follow these instructions to create the tree, rocks, and grass. The tree and grass on my landscape are machine embroidered designs. The rocks were trimmed out of a fabric of printed rocks and stitched with a zigzag stitch and monofilament thread. If you don't have an embroidery machine, you can make a tree similar to the one in this picture.

1 Cut a tree trunk out of brown fabric. Use the tree trunk at right as a guide to draw your own pattern.

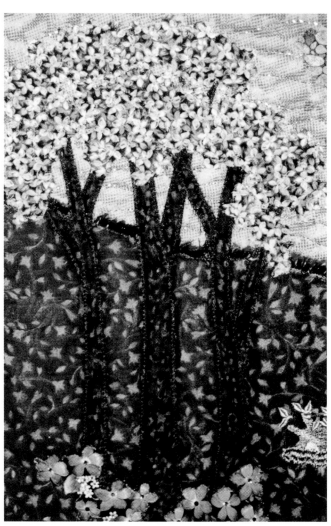

This is a simple technique for making a tree if you don't have an embroidery machine.

This is an example of a tree trunk with fabric patches layered over the tree.

2 Cut four fabric patches from a small floral print or green fabric that looks like foliage.

When positioned on the top of the tree trunk, these patches create the look of leaves.

3 Position the four fabric patches on the ends of the tree trunks, creating the look of foliage. Stitch the tree and patches in place with a zigzag stitch and monofilament thread.

If you prefer the winter look, don't add foliage.

4 Duplicate the rocks by cutting out basic shapes from several different shaded or mottled fabrics. Layer the shapes and stitch them in place with a zigzag stitch using monofilament thread.

These rocks were created by layering fabric shapes. The grass around the rocks and tigers was thread painted.

5 Thread paint some grass around the tree with a free-motion stitch. Drop the feed dog on your machine and gently move the fabric back and forth to paint the grass with the needle on your sewing machine.

6 Refer to page 102 for instructions for squaring up the landscape.

Landscape Tip

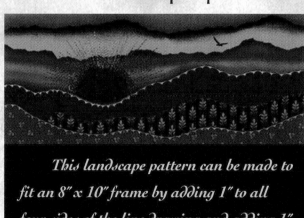

This landscape pattern can be made to fit an 8" x 10" frame by adding 1" to all four sides of the line drawing and adding 1" to the straight ends of all the pattern pieces except Mountain #4. Cut the strip of fabric for the sky 5" x 11". This enlarges the pattern line drawing from 7" x 9" to 9" x 11". In this case, cut the size of your muslin and stabilizer 9" x 11" and trim the landscape to 8" x 10" (1/2" on each side) once the construction is finished.

River Bend Line Drawing

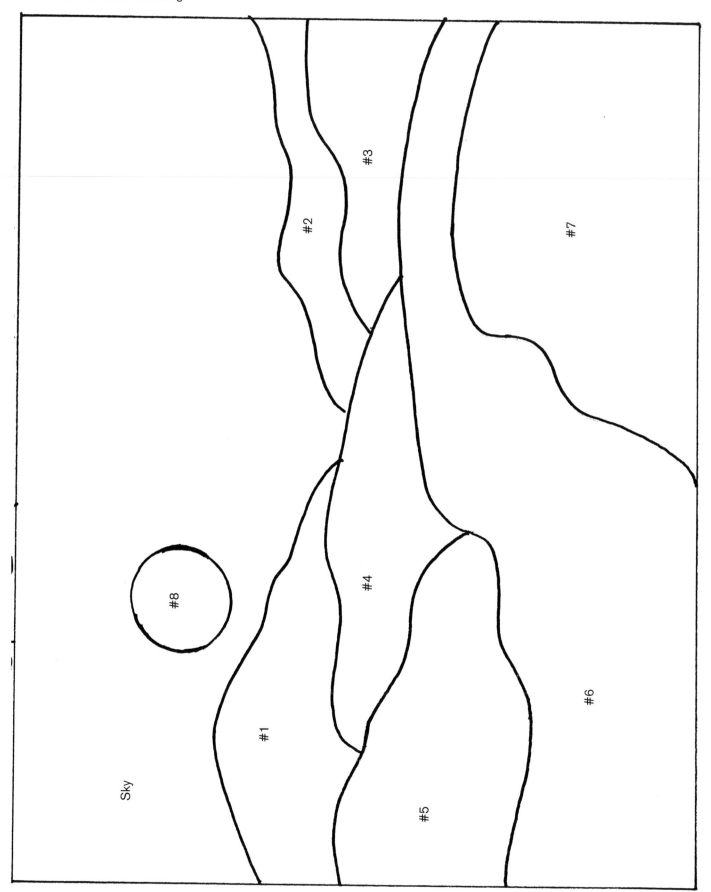

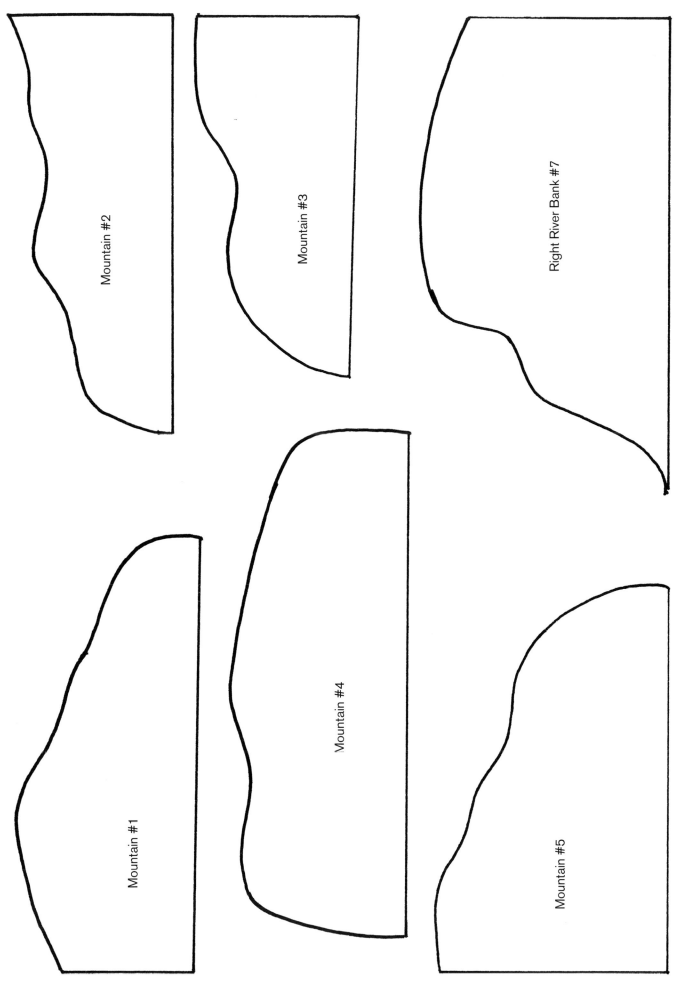

Mountain #2

Mountain #3

Right River Bank #7

Mountain #1

Mountain #4

Mountain #5

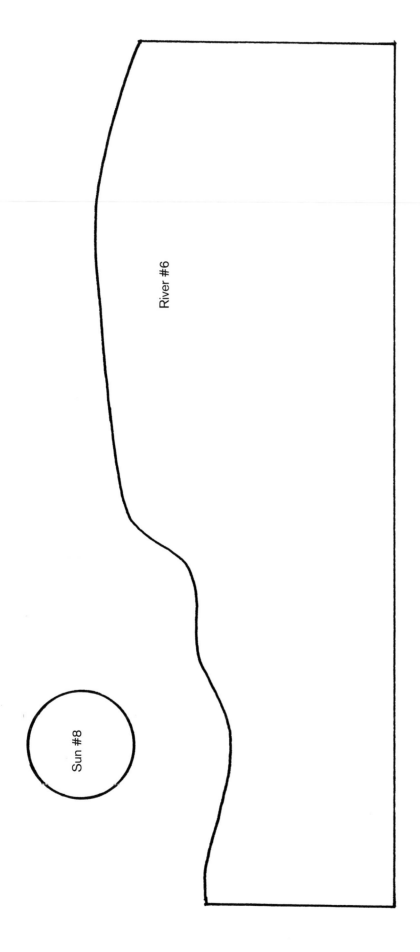

River #6

Sun #8

This is a very easy pattern to work for a full-size landscape.

Patterns for the "Smooth Sailing" landscape and the Pleated Prairie Points vest are on the pull-out pattern sheet in the back of the book. If you don't want to make the vest, "Smooth Sailing" can be quilted for a wall hanging or framed as a picture. Construct the landscape on a piece of muslin, then finish it according to what you have determined to be the end use. Refer to the construction directions for "Sail Away" on page 81 for step-by-step photos of the construction process. Refer to Chapter 10, The Finishing Details, for finishing directions.

To use "Smooth Sailing" on the back of the Pleated Prairie Points Vest, you will first need to determine the finished length of the back panel. The pattern is large enough to fit up to a size 3X and is 24″ long, which is the length of the vest. If you are going to lengthen your vest, make the landscape longer by either adding more fabric to the sky or bottom piece, or by placing a yoke at the top of the sky. Step-by-step instructions for the vest are on page 108.

MATERIALS

12 different fabrics (sky, sun, water, sailboat, 8 pattern pieces):

1/4 yd. each of 4 different fabrics for pieces #4, #5, #7, & #8

1/8 yd. each of 4 different fabrics for pieces #1, #2, #3, & #6

9″ x 20″ strip for sky (Note: to lengthen your landscape, add extra length for the sky)

5″ x 20″ strip for the water

3-1/2″ square for the sun

3-1/2″ square for the sailboat

(2) 3-1/2″ squares paper-backed fusible web (1 for sailboat, 1 for sun)

1 yd. muslin

1 yd. Stitch-N-Tear stabilizer (full sheet)

1/2 yd. cotton batting to put under the water and foreground

Thread to match or contrast as desired

Metallic or Sliver thread for stitching waves

Pins or temporary spray adhesive

Cutting Instructions

1 Cut out the landscape pattern pieces from the pattern pullout in the back of the book. You will use the line drawing of the landscape for positioning only. Since the line drawing is printed on tissue paper, it will be semi-transparent so you can see through it for positioning.

2 Pin pieces #1, #2, #3, #4, #5, #6, #7, and #8 on fabrics of choice and cut one of each.

3 Fuse a 3-1/2″ square of paper-backed web to the back of the 3-1/2″ square of fabric for the sun. (*Note:* if you are using lamé for the sun, fuse it first with tricot knit interfacing and a cool iron.) Leave on the paper. Trace the circle for the sun on the paper side of the square and cut it out.

4 Fuse a 3-1/2″ square of paper-backed web to the back of the 3-1/2″ square of fabric for the sailboat. Leave on the paper. Trace the sailboat on the paper side of the boat. Cut out the two boat pieces. On the paper side of the sail for the boat, use a pencil or pen to draw the dotted cutting line on the sail shown on the pattern.

5 Cut a piece of muslin and stabilizer slightly bigger than the back panel of the vest. Adding 1″ on all four sides, the approximate measurement is 23″ x 26″.

Construct the Landscape

1 Pin the muslin on top of the stabilizer (you can use temporary spray adhesive instead of pins if you prefer).

2 Lay the sky fabric strip on top of the muslin, lining up the raw edges along the top and sides. Pin or spray in place.

3 Use the line drawing as a guide to position piece #1. Pin or spray in place. Do not sew yet.

4 Use the line drawing to position piece #2. Pin or spray in place. Do not sew yet.

5 Position the sun where you want it. I tucked mine behind pieces #1 and #2. Remove the paper from the sun and fuse the sun in place. The iron should be set at a temperature recommended by the instructions for the fusible web.

6 Stitch across the top edge of pieces #1 and #2. I used a zigzag satin stitch for the construction of the whole landscape. You may use any stitch of your choice.

7 Stitch around the rays around the sun. See instructions on page 74.

8 Use the line drawing to position piece #3. Stitch across the top edge.

9 Use the line drawing to position the strip of fabric for the water over piece #3. Measure down from the top of the sky to the water line on both ends. This measurement should be the same on both ends to make sure the water is level. Use a satin ziazag stitch and stitch a straight line along the top of the water fabric, catching the top 1/8″ edge of the water fabric.

10 Position piece #4 over the water, using the line drawing for positioning. Stitch across the top edge with a satin zigzag stitch.

11 Use the line drawing to position piece #5 over piece #4 and stitch in place along the top edge.

12 Use the line drawing to position piece #6 over piece #5 and stitch in place along the top edge.

13 Use the line drawing to position piece #7 over piece #6 and stitch in place along the top edge.

14 Use the line drawing to position piece #8 over piece #7 and stitch in place along the top edge. Use a narrow satin zigzag stitch (2.0 width and 0.5 length) and stitch along both sides of piece #8.

15 For the sailboat, clip on the dotted line of the sail up to the top of the sail at the tip, but not through the sail. Leave a few threads at the tip, so that when you split the sail, the threads will act as a hinge.

You may add flowers on the foreground by using a machine embroidery design. Or cut some patches of flowers from a floral print and zigzag them in place with monofilament thread. See the instructions on pages 63 and 64.

If you are using the landscape for a vest back or a quilted landscape, remove the stabilizer on the back of the landscape. Be very careful when you are removing the stabilizer so you don't rip the stitches. The step-by-step instructions for the vest are on page 108.

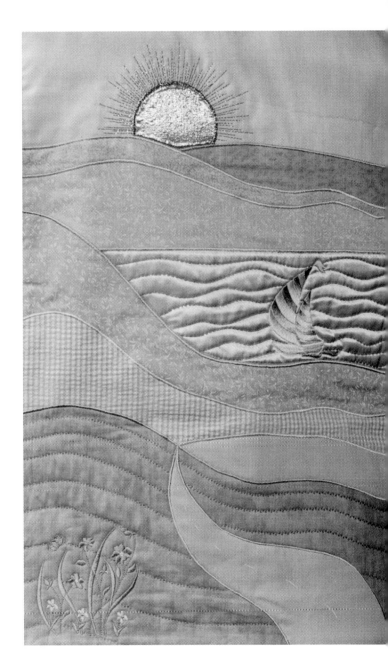

Chapter 10

The Finishing Details

*t*he finishing process is like the icing on the cake. A cake always looks and tastes much better when it is frosted. The landscape you have just constructed and embellished deserves to be finished in a way that showcases your work. I have been pleasantly surprised many times by how wonderful a landscape looks after it has been framed or quilted or sewn on a garment. It is kind of like magic—your creative endeavor suddenly appears to have had new life breathed into it.

No matter how you feel about the quality of your workmanship, please take the time to finish it well. A landscape never looks too attractive when you are looking at the raw edges around the outside. Whether you are framing the landscape as a picture, quilting it for a wall hanging, or sewing it on a garment, doing these final steps will be well worth the effort.

Square Up the Landscape

To square up your landscape, I find it easiest to lay the landscape on a gridded rotary cutting mat. If there is a water line, use that as your parallel line for squaring. If not, mark a parallel line across the bottom of the landscape to use as a guideline.

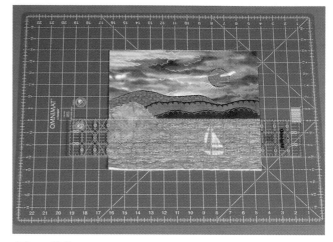

The grid lines on a rotary cutting mat are perfect for squaring up your landscape.

1 Use a straight edge ruler that is longer than the landscape is wide (you may need a yardstick). Line the ruler up across the water line, then make sure the ends of the ruler are parallel with the same line on the cutting mat.

2 Use disappearing ink or chalk to mark cut lines on all four sides. Measure from top to bottom, side to side, and diagonally in both directions. The top and bottom should measure the same, both sides should measure the same, and both diagonals should measure the same.

3 Use a rotary cutter to trim the landscape on all four sides, making sure it is square.

Framing

For landscapes 8″ x 10″ and under, square up the landscape to the size of the picture frame and place it in the frame. If the landscape lays nice and flat, you may not need to remove the stabilizer underneath. If the landscape needs extra support to keep it flat, mount it on a "sticky board."

You may want to use one or more mat boards around your picture or use the frame alone. There are many ready-cut mat boards available in numerous colors for standard-sized picture frames.

It is a personal choice whether you want to put the glass in the frame. I prefer to view the landscapes without the glass because I like to see all the detail clearly, but if the landscape will hang in an area where there may be steam or smoke, it's better to protect it with glass.

If the landscape is larger than 8″ x 10″, remove the stabilizer from the back if possible (sometimes the stabilizer causes wrinkles in the fabric on the right side). You can have a professional framing shop custom frame your artwork or you can do it yourself. In either case, sew 3″ strips of fabric around all four sides of the landscape. The strips are important for aiding in the stretching process as well as for securing the landscape on the frame board. The fabric for the strips can be scraps of leftover fabrics or pieces of muslin—they won't show on the finished piece. Overlap the edge of the strip 1/4″ on the landscape and zigzag in place.

There are many ready-made picture frames available at art and craft stores. When choosing

This landscape is an 8″ x 10″ pattern, but was enlarged to 11″ x 14″ by adding a mat board and frame.

a frame, you will obviously want to coordinate the frame color with the colors in the landscape, but don't forget to consider the color of the wall where the landscape will hang. I always try to choose a frame that will contrast with the wall. Otherwise it may blend in with the wall. The size of the frame can be slightly larger than your landscape if you are going to use one or more mat boards around the picture.

You may have the mat boards cut to size at your local frame shop. It is less expensive to purchase a ready-made frame and have the mats cut than it is to have the piece professionally framed. When choosing mats, use colors that are in the landscape. The mat choices should enhance the landscape, not take away from it. The objective is to draw the eye into the landscape, so be careful not to use colors that draw attention to the mat instead.

I mount my landscapes on 1/4″ foam core boards. These may be purchased at office or craft supply stores. Lay the landscape right side down on the table and then position the foam core board squarely in the middle of the landscape. Measure around all sides to make sure it is even. Stretch the landscape taut and push some T-pins into the sides of the foam core board. Wrap the fabric strips to the back of the board and tape them in place. Insert the covered foam core board in the frame.

If you are purchasing a ready-made frame, there are a couple of things to take into consideration. If you are planning to use glass, some of the large ready-made picture frames (16″ x 20″ and up) are not strong enough to hold glass. A frame that is constructed from hardwood will be durable enough to hold the glass. However, beware of a frame that is made from a soft wood that you can easily push your fingernail into. This type of frame is not strong enough for glass. If the frame comes with glass, of course it will be suitable. Also, check to see that there is enough room in the depth of the frame to hold the glass and the landscape.

Quilting

To use your landscape as a quilted wall hanging, first square it up (see page 102). Remove all the stabilizer on the back if possible. If you want to add borders around the quilt, sew them on at this time. I usually add two to three borders around the outside.

Cut a piece of backing fabric and a piece of batting 2″ longer and wider than the landscape (with borders attached). Place the backing fabric right side down on a table, then lay the batting on top of it. Lay the landscape right side up on top of the batting and center it in the middle. You should have 1″ extra around all four sides. Pin the layers together.

The borders around this quilt enhance the landscape and draw the eye into the picture.

Machine quilt the landscape using monofilament thread in the needle. The best way to do this is to outline stitch along some of the curves in the landscape using a straight stitch with a stitch length of about 2.5. I don't quilt every landscape piece, just four or five places at random from the top to the bottom.

If you added borders, stitch in the ditch along the seam lines of the borders. This is an important step to insure that the landscape won't fall away from the backing fabric when it is hanging. After you have finished the quilting, trim away the excess backing and batting fabric. Check again to make sure the landscape is square.

Finish the landscape with your favorite method of binding and include a rod pocket at the top for hanging.

Sewing a Landscape Into a Garment

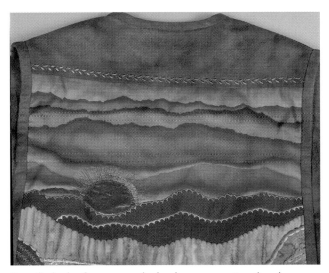

I used the landscape as the back pattern piece for the garment.

The landscapes in this book are sewn *into* garments, not *onto* them. That means I started with a pattern and used the landscape as the fabric for the vest or jacket back. Any pattern will work if it has a full back piece without a center back seam. I have a line of patterns that are designed especially to be a canvas for embellishments and also work beautifully for landscape backs (see Resources, page 128).

Remove as much of the stabilizer on the back of the landscape as possible. There may be heavily stitched areas where it will be difficult to remove, such as the water area. Removing the stabilizer is necessary to give your garment a softer hand, otherwise it will feel and look like a stiff board on your back!

Your pattern piece for the back may only be half of the back, because it is supposed to be placed on the fold line of the fabric when cutting. If so, cut a new full-size back pattern piece that is semi-transparent so you can see through it. Draw the straight of grain line down the center of the back. Then draw a second line perpendicular to the straight of grain line on your pattern. This line will help you position the water line on the landscape to make sure it's level on the garment. We don't want any lakes to look like they are spilling!

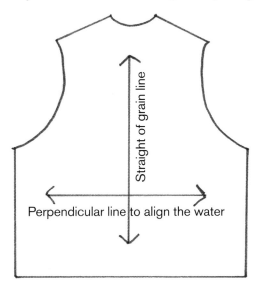

Straight of grain line

Perpendicular line to align the water

Lay the back pattern piece over the landscape to see how it fits. If the landscape is shorter from top to bottom than the back pattern piece, add a strip of fabric to the top of the sky to make the yoke. For best results, use a yoke fabric that is not very busy and coordinates with both the garment fabric and the landscape fabrics. You may want to fuse interfacing to the back of the yoke to give it more body. Topstitch with a decorative stitch just above the seam line on the yoke you added.

If the landscape isn't wide enough from side to side, add a strip of the garment fabric on each side. Use the same fabric as for the yoke. Again, you may want to fuse interfacing to the strips of fabric for extra body. Pin the strips along the sides of the landscape, right sides together, and sew a 1/2″ seam. Press the strips out toward the side seams of the garment back. Topstitch with a decorative stitch along the seam line, on the strip of fabric that you added, the same as the yoke above.

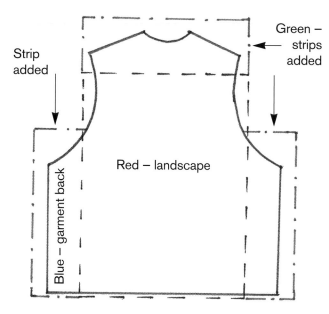

Lay the back pattern piece over the landscape. Make sure the water line on the landscape runs parallel with the perpendicular line you drew on your pattern. You may want to measure from the water line on the landscape at both ends, to the perpendicular line on the pattern to make sure these measurements are the same. This will assure that the lake is level on the garment and that it doesn't look like it is spilling. Cut out the garment back.

If the garment doesn't have a lining, you may want to cut a second back piece from another fabric to cover the wrong side of the landscape. I suggest using a lining fabric. Pin the two backs together, wrong sides together, and baste around the edges. It wouldn't be too attractive to look inside your garment and see all the stitching of the landscape construction. Treat the back as one piece and finish the garment according to the pattern instructions.

I have really enjoyed wearing my landscape jackets. I have commented many times, that I am probably the only sewing educator who gets more requests for pictures of my backside than my front!

Sewing a Landscape on a Ready-Made Garment

If you want to put the landscape on the back of a ready-made garment, here are the directions for how to do it. Choose a jacket, vest, or shirt that has a flat back panel without darts and very little fitting—a boxy style. The garment can be with or without a collar.

Make a Simple Pattern

1 Lay the back of the garment face up on the table and smooth and flatten as much as possible.

2 Cut a piece of semi-transparent tracing paper or tissue the length and width of the garment back. Lay the tracing paper or tissue over the garment and trace the seam line across the shoulders and around the neckline. Draw a new line 1/2″ above your tracing of the seam line at the shoulders and around the neckline. Trim your pattern tissue on this new line at the shoulders and the neck.

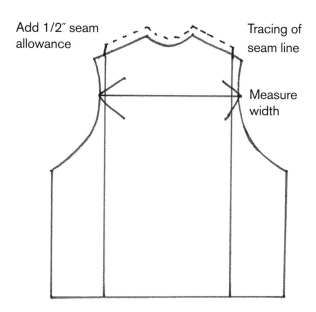

3 Fold your tracing for the back pattern in half along the center back, matching the shoulder points and shoulder seams. Measure the width of the garment back, between the shoulders, at the *narrowest* point. If this measurement is less than 17″, which is the finished width of the landscape, your landscape will need to be trimmed on the sides. To determine how much to trim on the sides, use the back measurement minus 1″. For example, if the back measurement is 15″, subtract 1″ for an adjusted width for the pattern back of 14″.

4 On the pattern back, measure from the fold line out half the distance of the adjusted width for the back. In the example above, you would measure out 7″ from the fold line, (which equals 14″ when you open up the back pattern piece). Draw a line from the top to the bottom on the back pattern piece 7″ out from the fold line. Cut your pattern on that line.

5 Draw a straight of grain line down the center, then another line across that is perpendicular to the straight of grain line.

Place the Pattern on the Landscape

1 Open up the pattern and place it on the landscape. If the landscape is shorter than the length of the garment, add a strip of fabric to the top of the sky the additional length that you need. Pin the strip, right sides together, at the top of the sky fabric and sew a 1/2″ seam allowance. Press the strip up and sew close to the seam line with a decorative stitch on the strip of fabric.

2 Position the pattern once again on the landscape and make sure the water line on the landscape is parallel to the perpendicular line on the pattern. Pin the pattern in place and cut out the landscape.

3 Stitch a piece of 1/2″-wide ribbon or bias tape along both sides of the landscape. Overlap the ribbon/bias 1/4″ over the raw edge and stitch with a straight stitch next to the inner edge. You may want to iron on 1/2″-wide Quilter's Edge (by HeatnBond) fusible adhesive on the backside of the ribbon/bias first. Then fuse the ribbon/bias to the landscape and topstitch close to the edge.

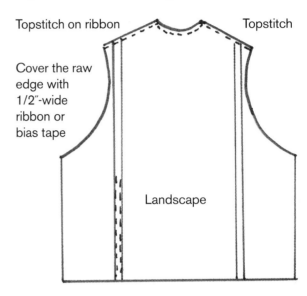

Topstitch on ribbon — Topstitch

Cover the raw edge with 1/2″-wide ribbon or bias tape

Landscape

4 Clip around the curve of the neck edge approximately every 1/2″.

5 Press under the shoulder seams and the neckline curve 1/2″.

6 Place the landscape on the back of the garment, and pin the folded edges of the landscape shoulders/neck next to the seam line of the shoulders/neck on the garment. Also pin along both sides of the landscape. Topstitch close to the folded edge of the shoulders/neck with a straight stitch.

7 Iron the ribbon/bias along the sides and fuse it in place. Topstitch along the outer edge on both sides of the ribbon/bias with a straight stitch.

Pleated Prairie Points Vest

Now that you've mastered making the landscape, embellishing, and squaring it up, you may want to make a garment to show it off. The Pleated Prairie Points Vest pattern in this book is a versatile pattern that can be used as a base for any type of embellishment. However, the directions in this chapter will show you how to embellish the vest front with pleating and tucking.

This vest was designed by making pleated tucks and embellishing them with decorative machine stitches, ribbon, and adding prairie points for the final touch. The tucks are blind tucks because there is no visible spacing between them and the folds touch or overlap the seam lines of the adjacent tucks. The finished width of each tuck is 3/4", which allows enough space to do the embellishments.

This reversible vest has a unique construction quality of exposing the seams to the outside of the garment and then finishing them with bias trim. This technique really sets off the creative embellishments on the panels in the same way a picture frame enhances a photo.

You can incorporate the pictured landscape, "Smooth Sailing" on the back of this vest, or use plain fabric if you choose.

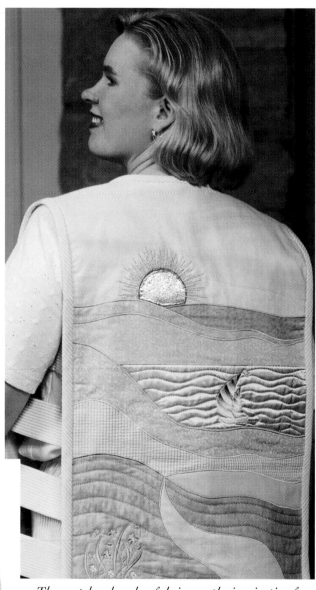

The pastel seeksucker fabric was the inspiration for this landscape vest. It is a very soft palette of pastels and I dyed the sky to go with it. Due to the soft mood of the landscape, I chose not to use decorative stitches, but just a simple satin zigzag stitch for construction. The instructions for making this vest follow. The instructions for "Smooth Saiilng," the landscape on the vest back, are on page 99. Full-size patterns for the vest and the landscape are on the pull-out pattern sheet in the back of the book.

MATERIALS

Vest fabric (45"-wide):
- XS, SM, MD — 2 yds.
- LG, XL — 2-1/4 yds.
- 2XL, 3XL — 2-3/8 yds.
- Lining fabric (45"-wide):
- XS, SM, MD, LG, XL — 1-1/4 yds.
- 2XL, 3XL — 1-3/8 yds.

Notions:
- 7/8 yd. fabric for bias binding trim

- 1/8 yd. each of 5 to 7 different fabrics for the prairie points
- 1/2 yd. each of 3 to 5 different colored ribbons 1/8"-wide to 1/4"-wide
- 5 to 7 kinds of decorative threads (rayon, metallic, monofilament, or regular)
- 1/4 yd. fusible interfacing
- 1/2 yd. Sulky Tear-Easy, or Pellon Stitch-N-Tear (removable stabilizers)

Cutting Instructions

Cut 8 strips of fabric and fusible interfacing for the side panels. Cut the strip size according to the pattern size listed below:

Size	Fabric	Fusible Interfacing
XS	5" x 6-3/4"	2-1/2" x 6-3/4"
SM	5" x 7-1/2"	2-1/2" x 7-1/2"
MD	5" x 8-1/2"	2-1/2" x 8-1/2"
LG	5" x 9-1/2"	2-1/2" x 9-1/2"
XL	5" x 10-1/2"	2-1/2" x 10-1/2"
2X	5" x 11-1/2"	2-1/2" x 11-1/2"
3X	5" x 12-1/2"	2-1/2" x 12-1/2"

General Instructions

This vest has a very straight-cut style, which you can shorten or lengthen at the bottom of the hemline. Determine how long you would like your vest to be. If you need to make alterations to adjust the fit at the hip line, you can do it easily at the side panel.

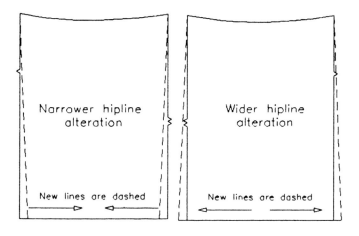

Narrower hipline alteration — New lines are dashed

Wider hipline alteration — New lines are dashed

The Vest Front

Create the tucks and embellishments on a rectangular panel of fabric. Lay the vest front pattern piece over the panels and cut them out. The cutting layout (see pattern sheet) allows for enough fabric to completely tuck both front panels. Using 45"-wide fabric, there are two panels allowed per vest front, which you can seam together to make a longer panel. Be sure to hide the seam, connecting the two panels together behind one of the tucks. Lay out the panels so that the straight of grain goes across the tucks for a flatter tuck. The pictured vest front shows randomly placed tucks between plain areas. You may embellish the plain areas with machine embroidery, appliqués, or other embellishment.

Make a plan of how you want to design your vest front or use the one below. Using 3/4" tucks, you will need to add an additional 1-1/2" per tuck to the total length of the vest front. Allow a few extra inches for the shrinkage that will take place in the tucking process. You may be more comfortable designing as you go by simply sewing a few tucks, adding some plain space, and stitching more tucks. I usually like to create my vests using the "design as you go" method!

If you are making a vest that is size large to 3X, the vest front has a bust dart. You need to consider this when you make your plan for pleating and tucking on the vest front. Plan to space the tucks above and below the bust dart. The bust dart on the vest front is approximately

12″ down from the top of the shoulder seam at the neck. Plan your pleats to fall in the upper 9″of the panel for the vest front, allowing plenty of room over the bust area to incorporate the bust dart. Start the pleating again 3″ or more below the bust dart. Trace the bust dart on your panel of fabric for the vest front. Sew all the tucks first, then sew the bust dart last.

Here is a sample plan of a vest front. I didn't incorporate as many tucks in the pastel vest shown in the photo. One side of my vest has 12 tucks and the other side has 13 tucks. You may add as many or as few tucks as you like.

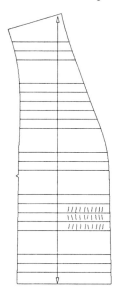

1 On the wrong side of the front panels, mark the tucks, spaces, and plain areas. Allow 1-1/2″ for the tuck and 3/4″ for the space between the tucks. Follow the plan provided or create your own.

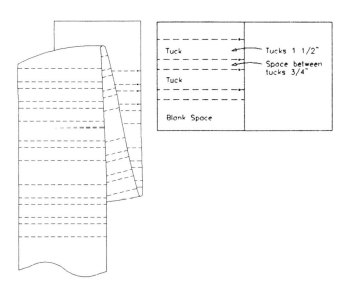

2 With the wrong sides together and matching the marks, sew the tucks. Align the fold of the fabric with the edge of your seam guide. Turn the previously sewn tucks away from the seam in progress. After sewing the tucks, press the folds, holding the fabric taut as you press so the tucks will lay down evenly.

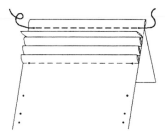

3 To embellish the tucks, place strips of stabilizer under the tucks and stitch across the tuck with some decorative stitches, sew over ribbon, or leave a few tucks unembellished. Lift the tuck away from the panel when doing decorative stitching so you don't sew the tuck down to the panel. Tear away the stabilizer once you have finished.

4 Lay the vest front pattern piece over the two tucked fabric panels and cut out the vest fronts.

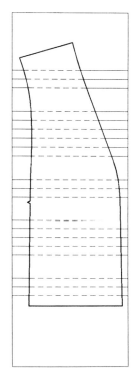

5 For the prairie points, cut 20 to 30 2-1/2″ squares from the contrasting fabrics.

6 Fold each square in half with wrong sides together. Fold the outside corners to the center, forming the point on the folded edge, and press.

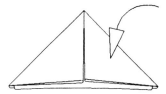

7 Insert the prairie points randomly under the tucks, with the raw edges next to the seam, and zigzag across the top close to the raw edges. You can place the side of the prairie point showing the folds either up or down.

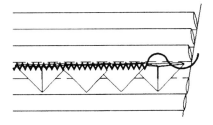

The Vest Back

1 Lay the vest back pattern piece over the landscape and make sure the water line on the landscape is parallel/level, then cut it out. Refer to page 105 for instructions on cutting the vest back panel from your finished landscape.

Making the Continuous Bias

1 Cut a perfect 26″ square. Mark the center at the top and bottom with a pin. Fold the square in half diagonally and press. Open the square and cut along the diagonal crease line.

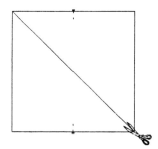

2 Pin the right sides of the triangle together as shown, matching the pins, and stitch a 1/4″ seam allowance. Press the seam open.

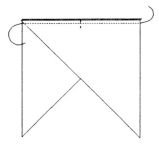

3 On the wrong side, mark the lines for the width of the bias (in this case 3-1/2″), using a yardstick or other long straight edge. Trim away any excess that is less than a strip in width beyond the last line.

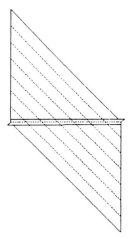

4 Pin the right sides of the parallelogram together to form a tube, having a marked strip width hanging off at each end. Make sure the marked lines match at the seam line and stitch a 1/4″ seam allowance. Press open. This tube will be slightly twisted.

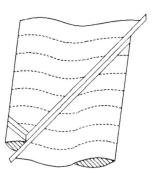

5 To cut the bias, begin at one offset end and cut in a spiral, following the marked cutting lines.

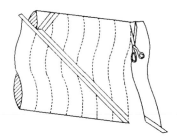

6 Fold the bias in half with the wrong sides together and press.

Vest Construction

1 With right sides together, stitch the vest shoulders to the back panel. Press the seams open. Repeat for the lining pieces.

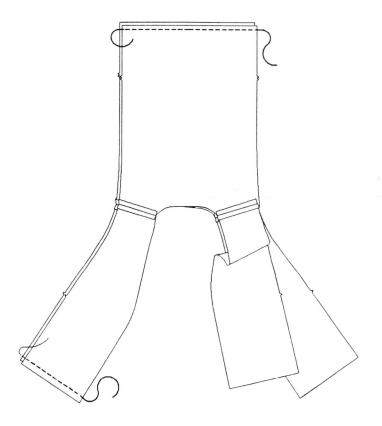

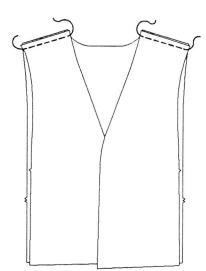

2 With right sides together, pin the vest to the vest lining at the bottom edges of the fronts and back. Stitch and press the seams toward the lining. Topstitch the seams to the lining only, stitching close to the seam line. Turn right side out and press again.

3 Baste or serge the raw edges of the vest and the vest lining together 3/8″ from the raw edges. The wrong sides will be together.

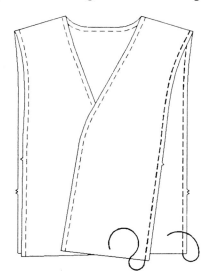

4 Fold the strips of fabric in half lengthwise for the side panel, wrong sides together, and press. Open the strip, and fuse interfacing to the wrong side of one of the halves. Fold the strip in half lengthwise again, this time with *right sides together*, and sew a 1/4″ seam allowance.

5 Turn the strip right side out and press. Pin the top and bottom strips 1/2″ from the raw edge at the top and bottom on the stabilizer side panels. Pin the middle two strips on the side panels, spacing them evenly apart. Sew the strips to the stabilizer using a basting stitch 3/8″ away from the raw edge along both of the side seams on both panels. The stabilizer side panel will be treated as though it is a regular side panel when sewing it into the vest.

Position strips 1/2″ from top and bottom edges

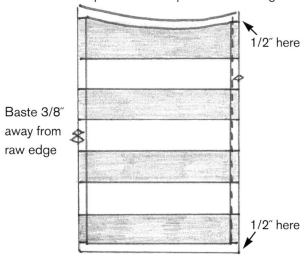

1/2″ here

Baste 3/8″ away from raw edge

1/2″ here

6 Pin the side panels to the vest front and back at the side seams, exposing the seams to the outsides of the vest. Pin the stabilizer side of the side panel to the lining side of the vest, matching the notches at the front and back of both of the side seams. Stitch the side seams of the panels with a 1/2″ seam allowance.

7 Tear away the stabilizer. Press the seam allowance on the strips to the outside.

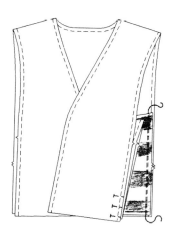

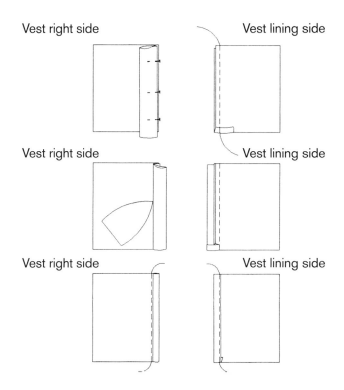

Vest right side — Vest lining side

Vest right side — Vest lining side

Vest right side — Vest lining side

8 Pin and sew the bias to the vest fronts and neck area with the raw edges even. Leave 1/2″ extra at the bottom edges. Press the extra at the bottom around to the inside and stitch. Press the bias away from the vest. Stretch the bias slightly around the neck and front bodice curves.

9 Fold the bias to the inside of the vest and pin in place. Stitch in the ditch from the front side of the vest next to the seam line. Barely catch the folded edge of the bias underneath. Press lightly.

10 Repeat for the side seams, enclosing the raw edges of the armholes and sides. Press the seams toward the side panels of the vest fronts and back. You can tack the bias at the bottom edges of the side panel or leave them loose. Pull the bias taut around the armholes to snug the garment closer to the body. This helps prevent gap-osis around the armhole.

The Landscape Gallery

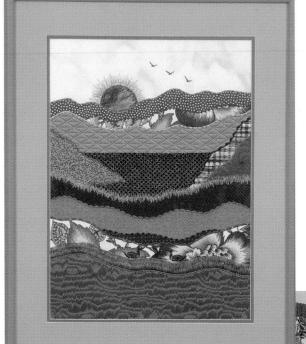

This landscape features the fabrics from my sunroom. It was a challenge to figure out how to include the large scale print that is the base fabric for the sunroom. I incorporated it in the second mountain from the top by showing just a slice of the colors. The print is repeated again near the bottom, but this time it shows a larger portion of the print since it is in the foreground area (second piece from the bottom). The water is a very unusual fabric because it is a piece of foiled dot sequined knit! It really has quite a sparkle from most any angle. The final touch is the stenciling of the ducks nestled in the grass and the birds in the sky.

The corner chair holds a pillow I made that incorporates the fabrics of the sunroom. The center of the pillow features a big red flower that is the largest portion of the design in the print of the base fabric. Because of the gathering in the window toppers, you can't see the full flower, only splashes of the colors.

"Stormy Day." On a recent visit to a friend's house, I found her with quite a collection of fabrics spread out on her living room floor. She was about to start making a landscape, but needed a few more pieces. As I looked at the fabrics, I realized I had the perfect sky in my stash, along with a few other possibilities. After we did some exchanging, I ended up with lots of new fabrics. "Stormy Day" is the result of combining two stashes. Check with your sewing friends—perhaps they will have something in their stash you might need.

Stormy Day has some interesting fabrics incorporated. The third mountain from the top with the fir trees has silver stamping on the fabric, which picks up a reflection of the silver lamé body of water. The far left lavender island that hooks into the water is actually a blouse fabric that has tiny leaves on it. I had to fuse stabilizer on the back of it to give it some support for landscape construction.

"Out of Africa" designed by Linda Crone and Betty VanBriesen, sewn by Betty VanBriesen. Betty and I enjoy designing together. We are a dangerous combination because what one can't think of the other one can! This landscape was a real work of love and took many hours of designing, sewing, and then determining how to frame it.

There weren't many decorative stitches used in the construction process, it's mostly thread painting, animal transplants from other fabrics, and machine embroidery designs. Many of the animals were thread painted. The foliage in the lower right corner was fabric that was trimmed out from another fabric print and transplanted in our scene. One border was added around the outside edge, and the landscape was framed by stretching it over stretcher board (thank you Mr. VanBriesen). This is a very special work of art!

Attending the International Quilt Market is a great adventure—you get to preview hundreds of new fabrics and products. "Visiting Geese" was created for Hi-Fashion Fabrics to showcase their new fabrics at their booth at Quilt Market. There were so many wonderful new fabric pieces it was hard to work them all into one landscape. To incorporate the geese in the body of water, it only seemed natural to cut around their heads instead of cutting them off to fit the pattern as it was designed. The foreground fabric looks like it has a meadow in the center section, so I machine embroidered a fawn resting in the grass.

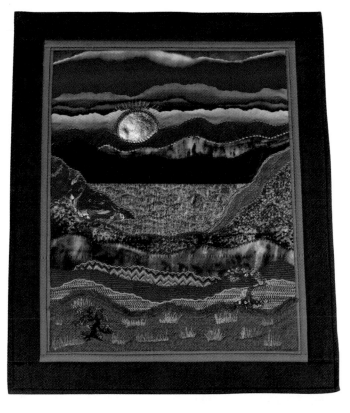

"Southwest Sunset" designed by Linda Crone and Betty VanBriesen, and construction by Betty VanBriesen. Several landscapes in this book have sky fabrics that are different color ways of the same print. This color way is a really dynamic sky for a southwest style. Betty accidentally discovered a new technique during the construction phase. The tree on the far right is the same tree as the one on the lower left. Our intention was to stitch the tree on water-soluble stabilizer so we could place it anywhere. As you can see, the tree ended up looking like a shrub after being dipped in water.

The water is actually a piece of upholstery fabric highlighted with bronze metallic thread. The tufts of grass in the foreground were done by free-motion thread painting.

"Florals of Provence" was created especially for a new fabric company, Michael Miller Fabrics LLC, for their booth exhibit at the International Quilt Market and their debut as a new company. The fabric collection in this quilt is called "Provence" and is one of their first releases. As you can see, these fabrics are cheerful, vibrant, and full of life.

This landscape is unusual in that the top two thirds of the landscape is one piece of fabric. It is a scene from France of gently rolling fields. I simply quilted around all the field sections with free-motion stitching and monofilament thread. The sections of flowers were cut into flower gardens and attached with free-motion stitching. The borders help to make the final statement by enhancing the landscape. Congratulations to Michael Miller Fabrics LLC on a wonderful new fabric. ("Florals of Provence," pattern #105 by Linda Crone Creations)

This animal quilt by Patsy Shields features a playful scene with animals "home on the range." The trees were highlighted with thread painting and the animals were machine embroidered. Patsy incorporated the fence and log cabin designs from my Signature design embroidery card.

Some of the fabrics in this scene are beautiful hand dyes. Patsy also incorporated some heavy textured yarns and a couple of gold ribbons formed into bushes. Great job, Patsy!

This delightful peach landscape quilt by Patsy Shields of Sulky has a very soft appearance, yet it presents a warm feeling. Patsy saw this scene in an Australian magazine and wanted to duplicate the concepts. I'd say she did a great job. The tree and foreground on the left were cut from fabrics that were crinkled first. Crinkling is the process where the fabric is dipped in water and twisted and knotted into a ball. Once the fabric dries, it is stretched out like an accordion and the back is fused with interfacing to hold the crinkles in place. Patsy added some topstitching to the tree trunk to make it look more realistic. The trees and shrubs on the hill were done with free-motion stitching. The flowers were composed with combinations of decorative stitches.

The fabric for this tote bag called out to me the minute I laid eyes on it. It is a Robert Kaufman fabric featuring a joyful print in primary colors. The landscape picks up the color theme by repeating the same colors throughout the scene. My daughter, who does not sew, was very proud of herself when she found this sky fabric and brought it home for me as a surprise. And a nice surprise it was!

This landscape was constructed first, then added to the front panel of the bag. Three different strips of fabric were layered around the landscape to imitate matting in a picture frame. The tote bag was constructed by applying fusible fleece to the back fabric for body and support. The bag has three zippered pockets and a color-coordinated lining! (Pattern #106 by Linda Crone Creations)

"Misty Meadows" by Betty VanBriesen. This delightful landscape was custom designed for a friend's living room with a soft blue and pink color scheme. This is a very peaceful and tranquil scene. The foreground features a machine embroidered baby fawn resting in the meadow with the butterflies. The body of water in this landscape is a piece of tissue lamé fabric. Lamé is very delicate and needs to be fused on the back with a fusible tricot knit interfacing for support.

This tiger purse is one of my favorites. The brown spotted fabric is a Debbie Mumm design and is the perfect backdrop for this scene. This is an example of a landscape that looks great without a lot of decorative stitches added. The simplicity is part of its beauty. It was stitched with a basic monofilament thread and a zigzag stitch. The tiger was machine embroidered and the birds in the sky were stenciled on. This bag was created in the same fashion as the tote bag on page 118. In fact, it is the same bag pattern, only this is square, more like a purse.

This pillow top was designed and sewn by Betty VanBriesen. A pillow top is a great canvas for a landscape. The base fabric for the backdrop of this pillow is used in the décor of Betty's guest bedroom. The colors are very warm and inviting. The tree is embellished with thread beads (refer to Chapter 8 on embellishments to learn more). The water has beautiful waves created with a Sulky iridescent thread that is a flat ribbon-like thread. It is an amazing thread because it picks up whatever colors it's stitched on. This landscape was finished around the edges with strips of the same fabric used for the pillow. The landscape was hand sewn onto the pillow top. You could add a landscape to any ready-made pillow using this same method.

"Rough Sailing" is the same pattern as "Sail Away" on page 80. Two landscapes from the same pattern can look so different with a change of fabrics. The fabric for the water is a fairly large print, but it looks great even in a landscape with smaller scale. The tree in the lower left corner was machine embroidered and little rock beads were sewn around the foot of the tree for a special accent. Framing is a crucial part of successful finishing details. Notice how the mat board and frame pick up the colors in the scene.

"Three Mountains" greeting card. I have a lot of fun making mini landscapes for greeting cards. They are so fast and easy. Because they are small, the size of the stitches and scale of the fabric prints need to be kept in perspective. I used a feather stitch with a stitch width of about 5mm, and smaller scale prints. The three mountains in the background have small running stitches coming down from the mountain top to create crevices. The size of this greeting card is 6" x 8", with a window opening of 4" x 6". It is a special die-cut tri-fold card called "Make It, Send It" by Linda Crone Creations. The landscape is glued behind the center opening of the card, then the back of the landscape is covered with one of the flaps for a clean finish.

The "Seagull Landscape" is a quick and easy project I teach at many of my hands-on classes. The sky fabric by P & B Textiles is just the right scale for this landscape, which is 8" x 10". A few of the seagulls were cut out of the sky fabric and fused over the water and mountain areas. The tree on the left was machine embroidered. The flowers along the bottom were created with stitches on the machine. The stems of the flowers were made with a feather stitch, and the flower heads with a "single pattern" heirloom stitch that looks like a flower.

"Lighthouse Point" is another tri-fold greeting card. This little landscape gets right down to the basics: sky, middle ground (water), and foreground. It doesn't get much more simple than this! The sky fabric is a small scale print by P & B Textiles and is great for little landscapes. The lighthouse is a design from my signature embroidery card. The fence was created by using a satin zigzag stitch for the posts and a triple straight stitch for the boards. The flowers are a combination of the feather stitch by using a narrow width for the stem and "single pattern" of a decorative flower stitch.

Here my daughter Tricia Bryant models "Blue Midnight" Fringed Cardigan Jacket, pattern #103. The back of this garment is a wonderful canvas for any kind of embellishment or creative work. You can find other patterns designed as a base for embellishment in the "sportswear" section of the pattern catalog books.

The landscape on this jacket is similar to the custom landscape created for Madeira shown on page 23. Since the jacket is longer than the landscape, I added a yoke to the top across the sky to create the extra length I needed. "Blue Midnight" has a lot of dark colors in it so I chose to use a fabric for the garment that would also be dark, and not take away from the beauty of the landscape. The navy mottled fabric looks like Ultrasuede from a distance, but is actually cotton. The front of this jacket has two of the landscape fabrics from the back incorporated into the piecing of the front yokes and pockets. These two fabrics are the leaves and solid green pieces you see at the very bottom of the foreground in the landscape.

I like to design landscape garments so the fabrics in the back and the front are related to one another. This helps create a balance in the look of the design.

This landscape jacket was designed around the blue leafy garment fabric from Robert Kaufman called "Blue Foliage." It is one of my favorite fabrics because I am very drawn to blue and green fabrics. The blue leafy fabric is incorporated in the landscape in the second mountain from the top and the bottom.

The sky has a few shiny iron-on crystal stars for accents. This landscape has two layers of batting under the foreground to give the contour stitching more impact. The front of the jacket was made with basic strip piecing techniques. The blue and pink strips of fabric were correlated in both the front and back.

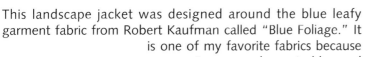

"Autumn Vest." The rusty brown and red flowers on the foreground fabric of this vest back set the stage for the colors of the landscape. The color combination is carried around to the front of the vest by embellishing with decorative stitches, frayed patches, and prairie points. The prairie points are also tucked in the hemline of the vest front. Just for fun, I laced dangling beads onto ribbon and chenille yarn, which were tucked into prairie points or threaded through a button. Pattern #101

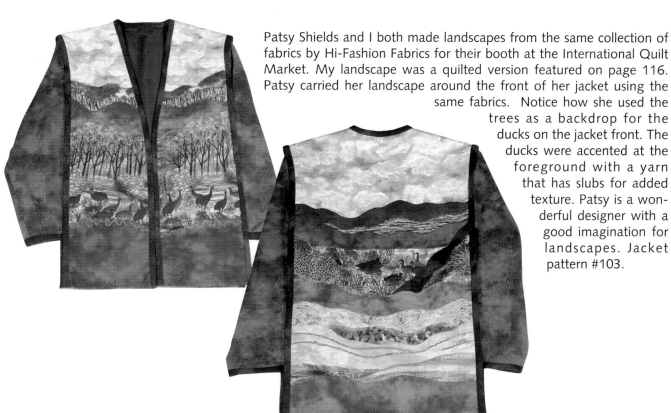

Patsy Shields and I both made landscapes from the same collection of fabrics by Hi-Fashion Fabrics for their booth at the International Quilt Market. My landscape was a quilted version featured on page 116. Patsy carried her landscape around the front of her jacket using the same fabrics. Notice how she used the trees as a backdrop for the ducks on the jacket front. The ducks were accented at the foreground with a yarn that has slubs for added texture. Patsy is a wonderful designer with a good imagination for landscapes. Jacket pattern #103.

This garment, modeled by Tricia, was made for Hoffman Fabrics' annual challenge a few years ago. It was one of the fastest garments I ever made due to a shortage of time. I chose the landscape colors based on the challenge fabric, which I incorporated in the second mountain from the top and the bottom. I also carried the landscape around to the front of the jacket on the yokes. On the left shoulder there's a machine embroidered tree with rock beads around the base. I stitched a strip of gold foiled leather along the yoke line for accent and laced it with a plum colored tube of fabric. This is Great Pockets Jacket, pattern #102.

This jacket is a duplicate of "Just Horsin' Around," a custom landscape created for Madeira shown on page 24. Betty VanBriesen did the construction. Extra fabric was added to lengthen the foreground, the horse fabric, in order to make the landscape long enough to cover the back of Fringed Cardigan, pattern #103. The horse fabric is by P & B Textiles and is called Naturescapes.

The mama duck with babies is normally a loon design from my signature embroidery card. By changing the traditional thread colors, these ducks take on a whole new look! The front of the jacket has some of the horse and rusty colored binding fabric incorporated in the piecing.

By Luetta Peters. Luetta says, "I loved making the artwork landscape jacket. It was a first for me. I really didn't think I could do it, but with the help and encouragement from my neighbor Patsy, I did it!" Luetta made two landscapes. One of them is on the back of the garment and the other landscape was cut into two sections and incorporated on each side of the jacket fronts. She has done a wonderful job of creating scenery and activity with the use of many machine embroidery designs. I really like the detail of the fence with the hopping bunny rabbits. The multicolored yarn was couched on the foreground and is a great touch for texture.

Nancy Wheat used the Fringed Cardigan Jacket (pattern #103) and the Peaceful Mountains landscape (pattern #104) to create her own one-of-a-kind winning garment for the Texas State Fair. Nancy is an artist who loves to paint and also does an awesome job of painting with fabric! Nancy combined some wonderful landscape fabrics in her scene along with lots of machine embroidery. Nancy chose to keep the stitching detail for the construction process more simplistic by using a lot of satin zigzag stitches. This was a wise choice because it allows the fabrics and machine embroidery to be the star attractions. Many of the machine embroidery designs were stitched with variegated threads. These threads really change the look of the designs, and are especially beautiful in the hot air balloon.

The front of the jacket combines many of the fabrics used in her landscape for strip piecing and the prairie points. Brown pine cone fabric provides a nice backdrop for the body and sleeves of the jacket. Congratulations Nancy, for a job well done. I am honored!

By Diane Miller. Great Pockets Jacket (pattern #102) and Peaceful Mountains Landscape (pattern #104) combined. Diane has done a wonderful job coordinating the colors in this jacket, and it has a soothing appearance. Blue and green are great comfort colors together. The batting underneath the foreground provides a wonderful base for the contour stitching

of the land done with a straight stitch. The fabric for the water is very effective due to the graduated shading in color. It creates the appearance of a reflection from the moon. Diane has also carried the same fabrics from the back of her garment around to the front in the strip piecing fabrics.

By Marge Albrecht. Fringed Cardigan Jacket (pattern #103) and Peaceful Mountains Landscape (pattern #104) combined. Marge's jacket makes quite a statement with the combination of fabrics brought together. She has done a nice job of carrying the theme colors in the leaves into the landscape. The sky fabric is a great piece for a night sky, and probably not traditionally thought of as "sky fabric." Marge extended the foreground fabric of the landscape to accommodate the length of the jacket. Many of the pieces of fabric on the jacket front strip piecing were also incorporated in the landscape. Using some of the same fabrics on both sides of the garment created a nice balance.

About the Author

Linda Crone has been an avid sewing enthusiast since about age eight. It was her entertainment as a child growing up in a small town in Iowa where there was truly "nothing to do." Sewing provided a way to generate income and stay at home with the children when they were young. And sewing played a big part in the homes she has renovated and decorated over the years.

Linda's true passion in sewing is designing landscapes and wearable art garments. She has been fascinated with the use of color for many years and enjoys using it to its fullest in the creation of landscape and garment designs. Linda has designed and published several garment and landscape patterns. Her designs have been featured on several television shows including "Kay Wood's Quilting Friends," "Martha's Sewing Room," and "Sewing With Nancy." Several of Linda's designs have also been featured in *Sew News* magazine.

Linda loves to share her love of sewing with others. She enjoys teaching, lecturing, and exhibiting all across the country at sewing trade shows, stores, and quilting guilds. Her classes and lectures are very inspirational and informative.

For information about Linda's patterns and products, you may contact her mail order service by writing to: Linda Crone Creations, 4832 White Oak Ave., Rockford, IL 61114. Fax: (815) 654-7558, Phone: (815) 654-9601, www.LindaCroneCreations.com, e-mail: LCCreatns@aol.com

Bibliography

Color Harmony, Rockport Publishers, 1994

McGehee, Linda, *Creating Texture with Textiles*, Krause Publications, Iola, WI, 1998

Fashion and Color, Rockport Publishers, 1995

Landscapes & Illusions, C & T Publishing, 1991

Machine Quilting with Decorative Threads, Martingale & Company, 1998

The Magical Effects of Color, C & T Publishing, 1992

Recommended Reading List

Adventures With Polarfleece: A Sewing Expedition, by Nancy Cornwell, Krause Publications, 1997

Beyond the Horizon, C & T Publishing, 1995

Complex Cloth, Fiber Studio Press, 1996

Crazy Quilt Odyssey, C & T Publishing, 1991

Dyes & Paints, Fiber Studio Press, 1998

Embellishments A to Z, The Taunton Press, 1999

Fabric Savvy, The Taunton Press, 1999

It's a Snap!, by Jeanine Twigg, Krause Publications, 1998

Judith Baker Montano's Landscapes (video), C & T Publishing, 1998

Mickey Lawler's Skydyes, C & T Publishing, 1999

More Polarfleece Adventures, by Nancy Cornwell, Krause Publications, 1999

Photo Fabrications, M.C.Q. Publications, 1999 (Distributed by Quilter's Resource Inc.)

Pictorial Quilting (booklet & video), Nancy's Notions, 1999

Point Well Taken, In Cahoots, 1996

Shirley Botsford's Daddy's Ties, by Shirley Botsford, Krause Publications, 1994

Shirley Botsford's Decorating With Fabric Crafts, by Shirley Botsford, Krause Publications, 1999

The Art of Manipulating Fabric, by Colette Wolff, Krause Publications, 1996

The Complete Guide to Rubber Stamping, Watson-Guptill Crafts, 1996

Thread Magic, Fiber Press Studio, 1997

Trees & Flowers Landscape Quilts (booklet & video), Nancy's Notions, 1998

Resources

Threads

Kreinik Mfg. Co. Inc.
PO Box 1966
Parkersburg, WV 26102
(800) 624-1928
www.kreinik.com
metallic, decorative cords & braids

Madeira SCS
9631 NE Colfax
Portland, OR 97220-1232
(800) 547-8025, free catalog
www.madeirathreads.com/scs
rayon, metallic, Glamour, Décor 6, Jewel

Sulky of America
3113 Broadpoint Dr.
Harbor Heights, FL 33983
(800) 874-4115
Speed Stitch catalog, free
www.sulky.com
rayon, metallic, Sliver, stabilizers, KK 2000 Temporary Spray

Superior Threads
219 Sugar Loo Rd.
St. George, UT 84790
(800) 499-1777
www.SuperiorThreads.com
decorative metallics, Glitter

YLI Corporation
161 West Main St.
Rock Hill, SC 29730
(800) 296-8139
Pearl Crown Rayon, Monet, metallic, Candlelight, silk ribbon

Sewing Machines

Bernina of America, Inc.
3500 Thayer Ct.
Aurora, IL 60504
(630) 978-2500
www.berninausa.com

Pfaff of America, Inc.
610 Winters Ave.
Paramus, NJ 07653
(201) 262-7211
www.pfaff-us-cda..com

Viking Sewing Machines, Inc.
31000 Viking Parkway
Westlake, OH 44145
(440) 808-6550
www.husqvarnaviking.com

Fabrics

Cherrywood Fabrics Inc.
PO Box 486
Brainerd, MN 56401
(888) 298-0967
hand dyed fabrics

Fabrics to Dye For
85 Beach St., Building C
Westerly, RI 02891
(888) 322-1319
www.FabricsToDyeFor.com
hand dyed fabrics

Hi-Fashion Fabrics Inc.
483 Broadway
New York, NY 10013
(212) 226-1400
cottons

Hoffman California Fabrics
25792 Obrero Dr.
PO Box 2009
Mission Viejo, CA 92691-3140
(800) 547-0100
www.hoffman.com
cotton fabrics

Michael Miller Fabrics LLC
21 East 22nd St., Suite 4C
New York, NY 10010
(212) 982-7919
cottons

Mickey Lawler's Skydyes
PO Box 370116
West Hartford, CT 06137-0116
www.skydyes.com
hand painted skies

P & B Textiles
1580 Gilbreth Rd.
Burlingame, CA 94010
(650) 692-0422
www.pbtex.com
cottons

Robert Kaufman Fabrics
129 West 132nd St.
Los Angeles, CA 90061
(800) 877-2066
cottons, denims

Rosebar Textiles
93 Entin Rd.
Clifton, NJ 07014
(704) 341-9780
tissue lamé

Miscellaneous

American Traditional Stencils
442 First New Hampshire Turnpike
Northwood, NH 03261
(603) 942-8100
www.Amtrad-stencil.com
stencils

Craftgard Co.
PO Box 472
Tustin, CA 92781
(888) 878-1212
www.craftgard.com
Quiltgard, fabric protector spray

Heritage Handcrafts
PO Box 261176
Littleton, CO 80163-1176
(303) 683-0963
stencils

Linda Crone Creations
4832 White Oak Ave.
Rockford, IL 61114
(815) 654-9601
www.LindaCroneCreations
patterns, Landscape Elements Embroidery Card, Make It Send It Stationery, stencils

Nancy's Notions
333 Beichl Ave.
PO Box 683
Beaver Dam, WI 53916-0683
(800) 833-0690
www.nancysnotions.com
sewing and quilting notions, threads, books, videos

Odif/J. T. Tracing Corp.
1200 Main St.
PO Box 9439
Bridgeport, CT 06601-9439
(203) 339-4904
www.odif.com
505 Temporary Positioning Adhesive

Omnigrid
1560 Port Dr.
Burlindton, WA 98233
(800) 755-3530
www.omnigrid.com
cutting mats and rulers

ThreadPRO, Inc. — Sew Zone
PO Box 487
Mabank, TX 75147
(888) 355-7646
www.Threadpro.com
ThreadPRO stand